The
Cactus and
Snowflake
at Work

The Cactus and Snowflake at Work

HOW THE LOGICAL AND SENSITIVE CAN THRIVE SIDE BY SIDE

Devora Zack

BK

Berrett–Koehler Publishers, Inc.

Berrett-Koehler Publishers, Inc.
1333 Broadway, Suite 1000
Oakland, CA 94612-1921
Tel: (510) 817-2277
Fax: (510) 817-2278
www.bkconnection.com

ORDERING INFORMATION
Quantity sales. Special discounts are available on quantity purchases by corporations, associations, and others. For details, contact the "Special Sales Department" at the Berrett-Koehler address above.

Individual sales. Berrett-Koehler publications are available through most bookstores. They can also be ordered directly from Berrett-Koehler: Tel: (800) 929-2929; Fax: (802) 864-7626; www.bkconnection.com.

Orders for college textbook / course adoption use. Please contact Berrett-Koehler: Tel: (800) 929-2929; Fax: (802) 864-7626.

Distributed to the U.S. trade and internationally by Penguin Random House Publisher Services.

Berrett-Koehler and the BK logo are registered trademarks of Berrett-Koehler Publishers, Inc.

Printed in the United States of America

Berrett-Koehler books are printed on long-lasting acid-free paper. When it is available, we choose paper that has been manufactured by environmentally responsible processes. These may include using trees grown in sustainable forests, incorporating recycled paper, minimizing chlorine in bleaching, or recycling the energy produced at the paper mill.

Library of Congress Cataloging-in-Publication Data

Names: Zack, Devora, author.
Title: The cactus and snowflake at work : how the logical and sensitive can thrive side by side / Devora Zack.
Description: First edition. | Oakland, CA : Berrett-Koehler Publishers, Inc., [2022] | Includes bibliographical references and index.
Identifiers: LCCN 2021032174 (print) | LCCN 2021032175 (ebook) | ISBN 9781523093366 (paperback) | ISBN 9781523093373 (adobe pdf) | ISBN 9781523093380 (epub)
Subjects: LCSH: Psychology, Industrial. | Personality and occupation. | Employees--Mental health. | Typology (Psychology) | Extraversion. | Introversion.
Classification: LCC HF5548.8 .Z19 2022 (print) | LCC HF5548.8 (ebook) | DDC 158.7--dc23
LC record available at https://lccn.loc.gov/2021032174
LC ebook record available at https://lccn.loc.gov/2021032175
First Edition

29 28 27 26 25 24 23 22 21   10 9 8 7 6 5 4 3 2 1

Book production and design: Seventeenth Street Studios
Cover design: Susan Malikowski, DesignLeaf Studio
Illustration: Jeni Paltiel
Author photo: Dan Corey

FOR EVAN

When you go out into the woods, and you look at trees, you see all these different trees. And some of them are bent, and some of them are straight, and some of them are evergreens, and some of them are whatever. And you look at the tree and you allow it. You see why it is the way it is. You sort of understand that it didn't get enough light, and so it turned that way. And you don't get all emotional about it. You just allow it. You appreciate the tree.

The minute you get near humans, you lose all that. And you are constantly saying "You are too this, or I'm too this." That judgment mind comes in. And so I practice turning people into trees. Which means appreciating them just the way they are.

—**RAM DASS**

CONTENTS

My Book Is Your Book

Hi. Welcome to my book. Make yourself at home.

What made you crease this spine? Are you plagued by a sense of otherness? Out of sync? Do you relentlessly process encounters until they are ground to dust in your mind? Harbor an uneasy suspicion you're hindered by a highly sensitive nature?

Or perhaps you live or work with someone who takes everything personally. An innocent comment turns into a tailspin. Drives you nuts.

I hear you. Either way, I'm here to help.

Some folks seemingly barrel through life. Don't look back, take it in stride. Ostensibly well equipped to navigate this world. *Roll-with-the-Punches* their middle, albeit lengthy, name.

Then there are the rest of us, exuding emotions, the smallest infraction permeating a not-protective-enough exterior shell. *What's wrong with me?* a familiar refrain. Second guessing = second nature. At times succumbing to the notion that those with a tough exterior are favored in the roulette of life. Not true. This misnomer belongs in the middle of a bologna sandwich.

DISPELLING MYTHS

A dozen years ago we were busily banishing false notions about introverts and extroverts. Believe it or not, back then some confused humans actually thought extroverts were somehow better equipped for networking.* We nipped that in the bud! Yet no resting on our laurels.

Our work is not finished. Now we're dishing about feelers and thinkers. Which will evolve into Snowflakes and Cacti.

Don't panic. I'll walk beside you every step of the way.

Perhaps you're new to the concept of personality styles. Is this uncharted territory for you? Here's a supersonic overview:

We each come equipped with particular proclivities, influencing our behavior, mental processing, and subjective experiences. Learning about predispositions yields insights into what makes each of us tick, heightens tolerance levels, and builds a platform to expand our comfort zones.

You've come to the right place for a slew of creative and actionable tools, tips, and applications. The best place to start is expanding your own self-awareness and fanning out from there to the world around you.

Own your temperament. It's as elegant—and often as elusive—as that.

---

* Zack, Devora. *Networking for People Who Hate Networking*, 2nd edition. Berrett-Koehler, 2019.

Laying the Groundwork

Life is short. Avoid causing yawns.

—ELINOR GLYN

JUMP ABOARD

Prepare to squash stereotypes, validate values, and dissipate erroneous judgments. Transform previously perceived liabilities into your finest strengths. In these pages you'll discover how to understand, accept, and leverage the true you. We'll address misconceptions and rewrite the playbook.

This is not about changing anyone else. Why bang your head against the wall? Expend your energy wisely; focus on refining you. Done well, that will take all your spare time.

From now on, we each get to define ourselves.

> ### DEBITS AND CREDITS
>
> My first semester as an MBA student featured a class in accounting. I had no idea what the heck was going on. Fortunately, I quickly befriended a certified public accountant (CPA). They were easy to spot, roaming the hallways with complex calculators handy. I arrived at my first tutorial with a single question: "Are credits good and debits bad . . . or are debits good and credits bad?" I was certain his reply would solve everything. He refused to commit to one side or the other. He said they are each good in different ways. Desperate, I started repeating my query louder, as a stream of tears began obscuring my vision.
>
> It's payback time. Fast-forward twenty-five years, and ever since I've been busily circumnavigating the globe teaching about personality differences. Again and again, I am asked whether thinkers or feelers are better positioned to lead, thrive, navigate. Opinions abound. Rather than offering up a pithy reply, I've been encouraged to write this book.
>
> Meanwhile, I eagerly await an invitation to scribe my first accounting textbook. Must be lost in the mail.

THE LONG AND SHORT OF IT

Here's what I know. There are ∞ personality styles. Or at least one per person, whichever comes first. A few may have a few, although that's an entirely different book.

Feelers value empathy, thinkers value logic, and the planet is filled with factions. *The Cactus & Snowflake at Work* demonstrates, amid a flurry of examples, why both sides are invaluable. Not to mention that we need each other desperately, despite ourselves.

Break It Down Now

If humans aren't complex, well then who is? (I know, I know, dolphins.) While keeping in mind that a heap of factors combine to make us who we are, this slender volume delves primarily into a singularly fascinating slice of personality. Yes, we are multifarious. Yes, personalities are intricate. And yes, by exploring even a single element we can forever change our understanding of ourselves and each other.

No need to bite off more than we can chew. Let's start here:

Thinkers lead with their heads and
Feelers lead with their hearts.

This statement encapsulates a basic underpinning of how individuals experience, make sense of, and engage in the world.*

The following distinctions offer up some highlights of our inner mechanisms.

THINKERS—LEAD WITH HEAD	FEELERS—LEAD WITH HEART
▪ Logical	▪ Sensitive
▪ Analytical	▪ Empathetic
▪ Direct	▪ Diplomatic

Thinkers are logical, value analysis, and default to directness in conversation. Feelers are sensitive, value empathy, and diplomacy reigns supreme.

Everyone has bits and pieces of both styles. The size and scope of these fragments depends upon each person's own inimitable inclinations. Fortunately, the exclusive *Cacflake Instrument*, a self-assessment nestled within chapter 1, has

---

* Based on teachings of Carl Jung (1875–1961), creator of numerous psychological concepts such as the four functions of consciousness, including Thinker-Feeler.

been designed to reveal your place in the world. Or at least along the spectrum of head and heart.

To kick things off, remember these truisms:

- Thinkers and feelers process life in fundamentally different ways.
- Sensitivity isn't equated with weakness. It's a superpower.
- Feelers think and thinkers feel. Everyone's three-dimensional.

Bonus point! Nobody needs to be fixed.

What to Expect

My style is casual; there's no hoity-toity pontificating. Yet don't be thrown by the chummy lingo—this volume is chockful of practical apps. All accessible without downloading to your over-tapped smartphone.

In my experience, engaging readers yields high retention. Therefore, you'll find an array of sections such as *Cheat Sheets*, *Dialogue Samples*, *Hazard Alerts*, *Pop Quizzes*, *Toolshed Moments*, *Worksheets*, and sundry surprises that I can't yet reveal. Or perhaps they don't exist (cue *Twilight Zone* theme song).

This book is replete with real-life scenarios to augment key points. Particularly robust scenarios are dubbed *The Rubber Hits the Road*.

All provided scenarios are based on *actual situations*.

Names and minor details may have been altered, yet the experiences and encounters described are rooted in true events. Keep this in mind, as I venture it will be hard to believe in certain cases. Truth is stranger than fiction.

A note about gender references. If you are reading this book in English or another language with limited gender distinctions, generic references to individuals are indicated by she/her, he/his, they/them, and related variations. Apologies in advance if unintended errors or oversights are made regarding gender identification and terminology.

BREAKING NEWS!

One more thing! From this page forward we hereby deem previously aforementioned feelers as Snowflakes. Thinkers are now dubbed Cacti. Done.

IS "SNOWFLAKE" (OR "CACTUS") AN INSULT?

Hi, Devora's editor here. (Actually it's still me; I'm only pretending to be my editor, since this aside was his idea.)

Some folks have a visceral reaction to the term "snowflake," as it has been associated off and on with negative connotations such as entitlement, intolerance, and inflated self-worth.

Likewise, while less charged, "cactus" has at times been associated with being harsh, abrasive, or judgmental.

As you'll discover, I use both terms as positive metaphors for contrasting predilections. This is not a book about culture or politics, but about personality and getting along together.

As an admirer of the inimitable beauty of both Snowflakes and Cacti, I reject turning either term into something categorically unkind or negative. So let's shake off any preformed connotations as we embark together into the light of these pages.

CHAPTER ONE

Traversing the Great Divide

TAKE A SELF-ASSESSMENT & EXPLORE THE RESULTS

Dream in a pragmatic way.

—ALDOUS HUXLEY

The ubiquitous snowflake ❄. An astounding meteorological phenomenon that floats, rather than plummets, toward earth. Featuring spectacularly nuanced patterns, snowflakes are luminous, delicate, and ethereal. Or that's how some would describe them. Others assess the very same mode of precipitation as fleeting, fragile, and frail.

Enter the cactus 🌵. Representative of an entirely divergent climate, cacti are sturdy, hardy, and resilient. Indisputably prickly, cacti epitomize a tough exterior. Uninterested in kumbaya, they prefer we keep our distance. To some this toughness is admirable. Others find it hurtful.

Human Snowflakes are wont to wonder *Why?? Why am I a Snowflake?* Such pondering does not plague Cacti. They merely go about their business.

There are challenges to surviving both the wintry tundra and the blazing desert. Ahead, we'll take tours of each, including what happens when the two cross paths. For we are surrounded by a random assortment of each style, resulting in a Cauldron of Confusion. And very few of us wear signage designating the nature of our preferences.

As we proceed, I'll share my dual intentions. Snowflakes, no feelings will be bruised. And Cacti, no time will be wasted.

A MATTER OF DEGREE

If we were all either pure Snowflake or pure Cactus, life would be a lot simpler. Not to mention, this book would be a lot shorter. You could start ripping out entire chapters! Slow down, speedster. As hinted at previously, there are not two cut-and-dried versions of disposition. Most people identify with Snowflake over Cactus, or vice versa, sometimes quite strongly. Everyone has at least smidgens of both primary styles. Plus, we stir into the mix all kinds of additional temperament components. It's a veritable potpourri of personalities!

There are degrees. Our natural nuances exist along a continuum. Envision an invisible silky thread traversing the terrain between desert and ice caps. It doesn't *have* to be silky, simply makes it more pleasant to wind around your wrist.

At one end stand a group of Cacti, tapping their feet, waiting for you to get on with it.

The other end is populated by a cluster of Snowflakes, politely introducing themselves to each other. These two groups represent those with strong preferences for one side or the other. There are also individuals a bit removed from these far ends, others edging toward the center with moderate preferences, and some very close to the middle, with slight preferences.

POP QUIZ!
The Quest for Correlations

Check yes or no to each of the following. Does a Cactus or Snowflake designation sync with:

TRAIT	YES!	NO!	CORRECT RESPONSE
Confidence			Nope
Creativity			Niente
Determination			Never
Fastidiousness			Nix
Independence			No way
Intellect			Not even
Leadership Acuity			As if
Organization			Nada
Resilience			Strike that
Sense of Direction			Jury is out

How'd you do? The upshot is that none of the listed traits are determined by whether one is a Snowflake or Cactus. The Snowflake/Cactus spectrum is a single aspect of our complex dispositions. Nevertheless, the implications are far-reaching, intertwined with how we experience life. It doesn't get more fundamental than that.

I call those with the strongest identification on either end *off-the-charters*. Those approaching the middle of our glistening thread present notably differently than their more extreme brethren.

While bearing in mind variations, this illustrious volume highlights the far ends of our continuum. This enables my gentle readers to best understand distinguishing factors of each style. We'll garner insights by focusing on these defining traits.

Tipping it another way, grasping the foundation enables attunement to more subtle distinctions.

WHO ARE YOU?

First things first. Let's discover where you land in all this.

You may get a kick out of taking the upcoming self-assessment featured in this chapter. After all, few things are more thrilling than yourself. Alternatively, the assessment may get on your last nerve. How dare I reduce your explosive personality into a handful of questions?

Either way, I will now commence to peer-pressure you into devoting a few moments to completing the survey. You'll be glad you did for the rest of this book and beyond.

There are no right or wrong responses and no good or bad results.

Assessment Instructions

Welcome to your very own personal style survey. Hereby dubbed the *Cacflake Instrument*. Free with purchase (shipping and handling $6.99).

Each numbered item offers two options to complete a sentence. This system enables you to indicate how strongly you identify with each option. Consider the degree to which the choices resonate. For each sentence pair, point distributions are 3 and 0 or 2 and 1.

If you agree entirely with A and not at all with B, assign A=3 and B=0. If you agree somewhat with A, yet more with B, assign A=1 and B=2.

Respond based on your natural point of view, not aspirations or adaptive behavior. If you engage differently at work and at home, answer as you are at home, in your natural habitat.

While there are three points to distribute for each sentence pair, half-points such as 1.5 are banned, under all circumstances! I run a tight ship.

The Cacflake Instrument:
Cactus & Snowflake Self-Assessment

1.	I deem a day well spent when	
	a. I plow through my to-do list.	_____
	b. I make someone's day with a kind act.	_____
2.	**If I am quite sure our paths will never cross again**	
	a. I don't particularly care if you like me or not.	_____
	b. I still aim for a positive, uplifting exchange.	_____
3.	**I collaborate best with someone**	
	a. With whom I feel a rapport and connection.	_____
	b. Who is straightforward and knowledgeable.	_____
4.	**I am**	
	a. Diplomatic.	_____
	b. Direct.	_____
5.	**I take pride in**	
	a. My intellect and skills.	_____
	b. My ability to notice subtle shifts in mood.	_____
6.	**I consider myself to be**	
	a. A person who leads with my heart.	_____
	b. A person who leads with my head.	_____

7.	Members of a well-functioning team	
	a. Feel safe and respected.	_____
	b. Have clearly defined protocol.	_____
8.	An admirable leader has	
	a. Proven credibility.	_____
	b. Genuine concern.	_____
9.	I aspire to have	
	a. A meaningful impact on others.	_____
	b. A notable impact on the bottom line.	_____
10.	Leading through challenge requires	
	a. Scrutiny and objectivity.	_____
	b. Empathy and compassion.	_____
11.	To establish common ground with others	
	a. I rely upon reason.	_____
	b. I rely upon compassion.	_____
12.	If I must give bad news	
	a. I provide relevant data.	_____
	b. I soften the blow.	_____
13.	I would describe myself as	
	a. Appreciative.	_____
	b. Analytical.	_____
14.	When making important decisions, I want to be	
	a. Fair and logical.	_____
	b. Sensitive and perceptive.	_____
15.	I value	
	a. Harmony and acceptance.	_____
	b. Accuracy and impartiality.	_____

The Cacflake Instrument:
Self-Assessment Scorecard
Be alert! These columns contain both A's and B's.

1	A =	B =
2	A =	B =
3	B =	A =
4	B =	A =
5	A =	B =
6	B =	A =
7	B =	A =
8	A =	B =
9	B =	A =
10	A =	B =
11	A =	B =
12	A =	B =
13	B =	A =
14	A =	B =
15	B =	A =
Totals (45)	Cactus =	Snowflake =

Strong Preference: 39–45
Moderate Preference: 29–38
Slight Preference: 23–28

Congratulations! You put the pedal to the metal and completed your assessment.

We will now dig into your *Cacflake Instrument* results.

Strength of Preference
You have two pieces of data to analyze—your primary style identification and the numerical strength of your preference. I suppose that summation is Cacti-centric. Here's an

alternate for Snowflakes: Now you can commence an exploration of your unique inclinations.

Spoiler alert! A strong preference does not indicate you have a stronger character than others, and a slight preference does not indicate any type of deficiency. This terminology is merely shorthand personality lingo, referencing placement on that recently discussed silky thread.

If your results total 42 or higher on either column, we can safely call you off-the-chart. You have a robust affinity for your dominant style.

If your results are 25 or lower for your dominant style, your results indicate you nearly split attributes of both types. No need to seek treatment; this is not indicative of a muddled mind.

Nor does it correlate with being wishy-washy or weak. I'd need to see you bench-press to determine the latter. Drop and give me twenty. (I do understand push-ups are not bench-presses.)

For your edification, following are summaries of strong, moderate, and slight preferences on each side of the spectrum.

Strong Preference for Snowflake

Land here? You have strong identification with virtually all the cornerstone Snowflake descriptors. Harmony, acceptance, and higher purpose are all intrinsic to your well-being. You seek meaning in daily tasks and encounters. Your inner circle will report that you also attribute symbolism to experiences that others breeze past. Acutely sensitive to conflict, feelings reign supreme. You care deeply about forging community and positive relationships. Perceived slights weigh heavily in your mind, and—if you were the inadvertent perpetrator—on your conscience.

Irrespective of a full schedule, you find time to help those in need. Heartfelt praise flows freely. In turn, you crave appreciation and revel in acknowledgment of your own contributions.

Moderate Preference for Snowflake

While a Snowflake, you identify with certain Cactus characteristics. You lead with your heart yet simultaneously seek a balance between values and practicality. Feelings outweigh logic in most matters. You strive to ensure decisions both make sense and buoy positive relationships.

You're a caring individual who moderates discussions by taking into account overarching constructs. Productivity and meaning combine to make you thrive.

Slight Preference for Snowflake or Cactus

Your assessment results indicate you identify with a combination of characteristics. You represent a near-even split between Cactus and Snowflake tendencies. We can deem you a Snowcactus. Or Cactusflake. Or whatever you suggest.

You can relate to a range of personalities with minimal effort. Your innate understanding of those who are both sentimental and hard-hitting leads to a natural ability to establish rapport. You have a propensity to bring people together, find common ground, and successfully facilitate challenging situations. Your gifts extend to coalition building and conflict mediation. Others can learn these skills, yet they come more naturally to you.

Moderate Preference for Cactus

You identify with many of the Cactus descriptors. You lead with your head and value being practical and fair. You understand some people are more focused on "touchy-feely" relationship-building. Competence is of supreme importance. When making decisions, you aim for fairness.

While giving positive reinforcement is draining, you make a conscious effort to do so, as it tends to up productivity. You place more value on telling the truth about what's really going on than being harmonious.

Strong Preference for Cactus

You identify with nearly all of the characteristics corresponding with the Cactus. Prickly is your middle name, and you're good with that. You are strong-willed and consider yourself a straight shooter—a badge of honor. It confounds you why folks don't leave their feelings at the door when entering a place of work—or anywhere, really. You're the first to admit a low tolerance for people who take things personally, particularly in a professional setting.

Praise from you is hard-won, as you believe people are paid to do their jobs correctly. You tell it like it is, providing direct feedback. You excel at analyzing situations and base decisions on logic.

Typical Response Patterns

1. "Wow. That's incredible! Devora is a mystic!"

    Because . . . the results convincingly align with self-perception.

    This is likely the case when:

    You strongly identify with one side of the spectrum.

    and/or

    You have previous knowledge about this facet of personality.

2. "Interesting. I can see how this makes sense."

    Because . . . the results more or less correlate with expectations.

This is typically when:

The results primarily align with self-perception.

and/or

You have a moderate preference on this spectrum.

3. "Kinda. But couldn't any result be interpreted as accurate?"

Because . . . you're close to the middle, one toe on the hot sand, the other atop an icicle.

This is often when:

You considered learned behaviors rather than inner preferences/temperament.

and/or

You responded conceptually, according to traits you aspire to and admire.

4. "This doesn't describe me."

Because . . . upon reviewing the results they appear inaccurate.

This can be due to:

Inhabiting an environment infused with many on the far end of your own disposition. Amid a plethora of strong Cacti, a slight Cactus may identify as a Snowflake in contrast.

and/or

A miscalculated score. This happens at times when transcribing your responses to the scorecard, as the A's and B's are not all in the same columns. This occupational hazard is outweighed by making it more difficult to "game" the system.

As is now evident, specific placement on the spectrum adds nuance to one's distinguishing qualities.

Gender and Temperament

You may be wondering whether gender correlates with temperament. Not necessarily, yet there is potential for stereotyping.

This risk is due in part to careless generalizations. There's a temptation to categorize Cactus traits as male and Snowflake characteristics as female. Furthermore, there is a statistical foundation for a degree of gender bias. Recent data is as follows:

Gender Data from U.S. Supplement to 2018 MBTI Manual (pp. 5–6)

MALE	FEMALE
Cactus (T)—68%	Cactus (T)—38%
Snowflake (F)—32%	Snowflake (F)—62%

Note: The MBTI Manual references Cactus as "Thinker (T)" and Snowflake as "Feeler (F)."

An uneven distribution on both sides of the spectrum is evident. However, there remain approximately one-third of individuals who identify with the opposite of stereotypical gender temperaments. There's a danger to classifying Cacti and Snowflakes as male and female driven types. Watch out for this tendency, potentially even within yourself.

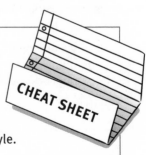

- Understanding ourselves is the foundation for comprehending others.

- We each have degrees of identification with our primary style.

CHAPTER TWO

Getting Acquainted

ROOTS OF STEREOTYPES
& REASONS BEHIND BEHAVIORS

When people talk, listen completely. Most people never listen.

—ERNEST HEMINGWAY

It's tempting.

You've completed your assessment and perused the results. Now, depending on your self-esteem and life filters (more on that later—see chapter 5), you're thinking one of the following (fill in the blanks):

I'm a _____, clearly the superior style.

I'm a _____, clearly the inferior style.

Either way, you're off the mark. Sorry, Flakers (a term of endearment)! I don't mean to hurt your feelings. I meant to say: Either way, you are a good person. Here, have a tissue. Cacti, I know we're good.

DEFINING CHARACTERISTICS

The differences between these two styles means we can get on each other's last nerve. For starters, why are you so callous . . . or sentimental? As we established, Cacti lead with their heads while Snowflakes lead with their hearts. What about related defining traits?

To assist with your admirable quest for clarity, I've assembled this spiffy chart:

	Cacti are . . . logical, analytical, impartial.
	Cacti base decisions on reason.
	Cacti value . . . consistency, accuracy, and rationality.
	Cacti default to . . . directness.
	Snowflakes are . . . sensitive, appreciative, involved.
	Snowflakes base decisions on feelings.
	Snowflakes value . . . harmony, kindness, and empathy.
	Snowflakes default to . . . diplomacy.

MEMORY REFRESH: A higher assessment result correlates with a strong affinity for this breakdown of flagship traits. A slight preference means you relate only to a subset of components on each list.

Let's delve further into clutch characteristics of each habitat dweller.

Cacti are *logical*, Snowflakes are *sensitive*.

I cross-referenced the definitions of each key word in a couple of highbrow dictionaries. *Oxford English Dictionary* and *Webster's* are my favorites. Though between you and me, they can get a bit verbose. The meaning of each key trait can be parsed into two definers:

LOGICAL: Rational, reasonable

SENSITIVE: Perceptive, caring

While Flakers tout sensitivity, logic prevails for Cacti. What are the implications?

To explore further, we'll traverse into that dangerous territory of antonyms. Risky, yet telling. Let's play a game.

POP QUIZ!
GUESS THE OPPOSITE

I implore you to not peek ahead; we'll have more fun that way. Fill the blanks in the "Antonyms" column with your best guess. Go with stream of consciousness.

PRIMARY TRAITS	KEY DESCRIPTORS	ANTONYMS OF PRIMARY TRAITS
Logical	Rational/Reasonable	
Sensitive	Perceptive/Caring	

Hold up! Refrain from peeking until you've written something in those blank boxes.

Research reveals . . .

Here comes the antonym of logical . . . incoherent.

And the opposite of sensitive? Superficial.

DESCRIPTOR	DEFINITION	ANTONYMS
Logical	Rational/Reasonable	Incoherent
Sensitive	Perceptive/Caring	Superficial

In other words—and words loom large in misfires—this is not about minor matters.

How Labels Lead to Judgment

When a Cactus remarks that logic reigns supreme, the stakes are high. Illogical is the equivalent of incoherent. The implication that follows is that Snowflakes are incoherent. A slapdash approach to life. That's a low blow.

If sensitivity reigns supreme for Snowflakes, then being perceptive and caring is the way to go. If you're not? Yikes. Superficial. A shallow approach to life. The ultimate Snowflake diss.

A solid portion of stereotyping is rooted in faulty analysis of others' behaviors.

Enter our first *Toolshed Moment*. Each of these gems introduces customizable processes or tools for your exclusive use.

TOOLSHED MOMENT
Busting Stereotypes

This model provides a systematic approach to address and dispense with stereotypes. They abound all around us. We'll examine a few prevailing heavy hitters, cull the so-called proof, identify possible roots, and assess their validity.

STEREOTYPE A: Snowflakes are wimps.
What's the so-called proof?
They mist up regularly. Even occasionally when watching a subpar commercial.
What's the root?
They are deeply sensitive. They intensely reflect upon events. They emote.
Is it true? Are Snowflakes oversensitive dolts?
This is an inherently flawed question—*oversensitive* is a judgment. Being an empath has tremendous value.

STEREOTYPE B: Cacti are jerks.

What's the so-called proof?

They can be unapologetically grumpy curmudgeons.

What's the root?

They cut to the chase. They're rough around the edges. At times they inadvertently offend.

Is it true? Are Cacti insensitive clods?

An incongruent tone doesn't equate with being impervious. They are frequently unaware of conversational nuances. A hearty constitution has tremendous value.

STEREOTYPE C: Snowflakes don't think things through.

What's the so-called proof?

Logical analysis is of no interest.

What's the root?

Feelings reign supreme.

Is it true? Do Snowflakes lack the ability to process?

Nothing could be further from the truth. Snowflakes relentlessly process events. As a Snowflake explained, "I give everything careful thought." They're constantly thinking things over. Especially their feelings. *Just kidding*. Kinda.

STEREOTYPE D: Cacti aren't driven by values.

What's the so-called proof?

They hardly ever mention their values.

What's the root?

Cacti's values are more behind the scenes, rather than at the forefront of each interaction.

Is it true? Are Cacti disinterested in guiding values?

Nothing could be further from the truth. Maintaining a strong set of guiding principles is as foundational to Cacti as to Snowflakes. They each just value different things.

Let's Save the World

Who do you suppose is most likely to save the world?

Snowflakes are madly waving their hands in the air, shouting "Me! Me! Over here!"

Take a number, have a seat. For starters, "saving the world" is a Snowflake phrase. The aspiration looms large in their minds on a regular basis. Cacti are generally occupied with more tangible matters, such as *Will this 2x4 fit in the back of my truck?* (Confession! I drive a beat-up pickup truck and was seeking an opportunity to weave that fact into this manuscript while simultaneously busting stereotypes.)

Let's be real. Despite being a five-star Snowflake, I cannot conscionably allow my brethren to claim they corner the saving-the-world market. There are many reasons. Here come two.

Reason One

Here's the rub. The intensity of Snowflakes' delicate feelings can thwart the realization of their goals. It's too sad, or overwhelming, or heart-wrenching.

Snowflakes *care* deeply. It's a badge of honor. Yet the harsh reality of the cold, cruel world can derail best intentions. A dismissive remark or perceived insult can be temporarily incapacitating.

Reason Two

Cacti are unhindered by emotional reactions. Many are scientists, engineers, mechanics, builders, attorneys. They are *not* jerks. That is an ungrounded judgment. I will not tolerate it. Some of my best friends are Cacti.

They don't really care about feelings. They're more cerebral. Cacti are practical and pragmatic. They get things done and are responsible for much good.

THE RUBBER HITS THE ROAD
Snowflake Student in Senior Home

Elana, a junior in college, decided to seek out volunteer work. She figured it would provide balance to her life while also making a positive difference. She never had the opportunity to spend time with her own grandparents, so Elana applied for a volunteer activity specialist position at a local senior home. A glistening Snowflake, she envisioned forging beautiful connections with the residents.

Upon entering the facility, she saw seniors parked in wheelchairs all over the place, most sitting alone. Convinced she could vicariously experience their despairing energy, her breathing became labored. The residents seemed displaced, disheveled, confused. Despite being in a highly regarded senior home, all she experienced was darkness and depression. Elana turned around and exited the facility.

Back on the sun-drenched sidewalk, she walked slowly up and down the street. After about twenty minutes, she pulled herself together. Slowly, she acknowledged she was projecting her own feelings. She also recognized a disconnect. How could she allow a sympathetic nature to prevent her from being a much-needed activities volunteer?

Elana marched herself back inside. Upon return Elana viewed the well-run home in a different light, realizing she had imposed her own discomfort upon others. She filled out the detailed application with aplomb.

Elana volunteered happily there for the next three years. What she initially experienced as overwhelming gradually became a peaceful part of her weekly routine. She soon embodied the benefits of propelling herself beyond an initial perceived limitation.

Understanding your natural inclinations can explain emotional and cognitive reactions without limiting your possibilities. Taking on a new experience was a valuable enough opportunity for Elana to rally and push through her initial hesitation.

REASONS BEHIND BEHAVIORS

By paying attention, we can make predictive observations. That is different from citing our observations as proof of others' penchants. It is rare to fully grasp the impetus behind others' behaviors. Equating behaviors with evidence of their driving forces is risky business.

Self-identification as a Snowflake or Cactus does not preclude either from a particular lifestyle or profession.

**Grasping the *reasons* behind behaviors
sheds light on inner natures.**

Let's look at four examples of how this can manifest.

Example One: Kindergarten Teacher

You encounter a kindergarten schoolteacher. Obviously, a Snowflake. Slam dunk? Not so fast. This job is filled by all types. The appeal to a Snowflake is perhaps what popped into your mind: caring for kids during such a pure stage in life. Snowflake early learning teachers would cite the privilege of watching children grow up under their tutelage, cherishing a job infused with purpose, and having a meaningful influence on lives. Cue string quartet.

Plenty of Cacti pursue the same path. What's the draw? They thrive on creating a structured, systematic curriculum, gleaning an ongoing sense of accomplishment, and maintaining an organized, safe environment.

Example Two: Religious Affiliation

Take two. Imagine meeting two equally devout people. Based on the lens through which you view religiosity, you may determine they are drawn to religion for similar reasons. And why not? They follow the same rules, celebrate the same holidays, ascribe to the same beliefs, and attend the same house of worship.

Dig a little deeper and learn about the underlying reasons for each person's affiliation. Cacti are generally drawn to the structure provided and the intellectual discourse of accompanying scripture. Snowflakes will cite their affinity for spirituality and honing interpersonal connections.

Example Three: Vegetarianism

What associations come to mind when you learn an acquaintance is vegetarian? Go nuts; no one will see your list but me. Come to think of it, barring an unanticipated revolutionary metaphysical phenomenon, I won't either. Particularly if you think up the list in your mind.

There is a pervasive proclivity to link vegetarianism with Snowflakery. Topping the list: being soft-hearted, emotional, and prone to feelings of guilt. Many of these factors do come into play with the reasons some Snowflakes avoid meat.

Yet Cacti are dedicated vegetarians for reasons other than feeling sorry for the animals or sentimentality. A vegetarian Cactus explained to me it is illogical to eat animals. As a doctor, he accrued data that a plant-based diet is healthier than one featuring meat. His second reason is rooted in ecology. Far fewer resources are required to sustain the planet and provide food globally on a vegetarian diet. He is motivated by reasons perfectly in sync with his Cactus nature.

Example Four: Yoga Instructor

Teaching yoga may seem to tip the scales as a Snowflakey job. Many classes start with an "Ommm" to connect participants' energy to the cosmos. Still, plenty of Cacti pursue this path. It would be hard for an outside observer to assess instructors' personas. Yet learning the reasons behind others' desires to become yogis would clear up the differences faster than a windshield in a car wash. You could also learn quite a bit by listening to their patter.

A Cactus Yogi is drawn to what is practical and measurable. Yoga offers a detailed, coherent system of linking body and breath. They emphasize structure, with precise movements to learn, and physical benefits, such as releasing tightness, strengthening the core, aiding digestion, and improving balance.

Snowflake yogis speak of entirely different matters. They remind you to transfer lessons from the mat to your daily life. They are apt to share inspirational quotes. A Snowflake will encourage participants to cultivate a community, emphasizing we are all part of a greater whole.

Targeting Motivators

Personality propensities provide insights to the motivation behind behaviors. And if you can target what drives someone else, you're on the fast track to stronger relationships.

"Hold it right there!" you interrupt. "What if I don't have a clue regarding another's inner machinations?" Nice try. I'm not *that* easy to stump. Reminds me of a recent conversation.

I was coaching a newly minted supervisor. Our discussion turned to the value of targeting other's motivators. He paused to take notes. After taking a moment to collect his thoughts, he concluded, "I need to figure out what they want."

I smiled, promising, "It's a lot easier than that."

No cerebral calisthenics required. Plus, you can circumvent consulting a Magic Eight Ball . . . although they can be rather helpful in a pinch.

If you don't know what compels others, I've got a sparkly two-part solution ready to go.

TOOLSHED MOMENT
The Big Two

The Big Two is handy in myriad situations. It's useful when making a new acquaintance. It is also helpful to steer a relationship back on course when it is veering dangerously close to the precipice. In fact, I'm hard-pressed to find a category of relationship that couldn't benefit from some version of this tool.

ONE: OBSERVE

You can absorb a remarkable amount by sharpening your observational acuity. Suggestions to get you started on your new quest:

- Listen deeply.
- Refine your focus on details.
- Note word choices and tonality.
- Take heed of slight changes in expressions.
- Pick up on shifts in physical stance.
- Notice when a face lights up.
- Observe infusions of energy during conversation.
- Look out for either diminished or increased eye contact.
- Pay astute attention to who is right there with you.

All of these are clues for what resonates with others. Yet what if you . . .

. . . are still uncertain? No worries.

. . . want to check in on your hunches? Good idea.

. . . have limited cues to draw upon? I'm with you.

. . . encounter a technological hindrance? Who hasn't?

Let's head over to:

TWO: ASK

It's astonishing how often this option is overlooked. Asks are far-ranging, including:

- Inquire about what energizes and drives people.
- Request information about communication preferences.
- Ask for examples of others' inspirations and motivators.
- Prepare to ask open-ended follow-up questions.

SUPPLEMENTARY TIPS

- Limit yourself to one or two questions at a time. Avoid emulating an inquisition.
- Give time for others to ponder their reply. They may need to think it over.
- Provide the option of getting back to you.
- Seek clarification. People have varying definitions of virtually everything.

DIALOGUE SAMPLE

Sandy, a Cactus and freshly appointed department head, has just met her new assistant, Lee. He's a Snowflake, although she's not yet aware of that. Besides working on her observational skills, she is also a big believer in asking questions. Following is a sample fragment of their discussion.

SANDY: I give feedback regularly; I think it's vital to professional growth.

LEE: Sounds good.

SANDY: I'm not one to mince words. Does that suit you?

LEE: Well . . . I might prefer it a little smoothed around the edges. [He breaks eye contact.]

SANDY: How might that play out?

LEE: Ummm . . .

SANDY: [Restrains herself from jumping in, giving him time to formulate thoughts.]

LEE: I mean, I want to learn how to improve. Yet I do think the way someone gives feedback makes a difference. I like to also learn what I'm doing right.

SANDY: I agree. How about we check in after our first session to see if we're on track?

LEE: [Brightens and sits up straighter.] That's a great idea.

What Sandy Modeled

- Noticing nonverbal indicators
- Requesting clarity ("How might that play out?")
- Exhibiting patience
- Building rapport ("I agree.")
- Offering to continue the process

Even with keen observations and thoughtful questions, sometimes we miss the mark. That's cool; it isn't a problem. Focusing and asking conveys a sincere interest. Putting forth an effort is an admirable—and typically appreciated—step forward.

And now a highly anticipated synopsis of advantageous perks and irksome propensities for each side of the aisle. After all, everything has its ups and downs.

PERKS AND PROPENSITIES

I'm glad you're on board that one personality variance is not intrinsically better than the other. Still, there are indisputable side benefits and challenges on each end of the spectrum.

A Few Cactus Pleasant Perks and Perplexing Propensities

They don't . . .

- Wallow

- Beat up on themselves

- Suffer from delicate feelings

They are . . .

- Low maintenance

Yet prone to . . .

- Have a prickly exterior

- Escalate conflict

A Few Flaker Pleasant Perks and Perplexing Propensities

They don't . . .

- Pick a fight
- Disturb the peace
- Hurt others' feelings

They are . . .

- Tuned in to emotions

Yet prone to . . .

- Take things personally
- Overread into situations

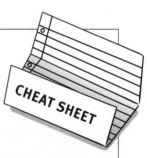

- Personalities are complex; there is more than meets the eye.

- Debunking stereotypes enables us to understand reasons behind behaviors.

- Not certain what others value? Remember the Big Two: observe and ask.

CHAPTER THREE

Respect

PLATINUM RULE, FLEX YOUR STYLE & MIND YOUR OWN BUSINESS

To handle yourself, use your head. To handle others, use your heart.

—ELEANOR ROOSEVELT

Wouldn't the world be a better place if we just buckled down and *respected* people? For goodness' sake, is that asking too much?

If only it were that simple.

Let's start with this doozy:

We are *not* all the same inside.

In fact, we're wildly divergent. That is why respect is conceptually tricky.

THE THEORY OF RELATIVITY

Einstein was right ... *again*! Besides knowing his way around a slide rule, Einstein had some great one-liners. I will go the bold route of proclaiming that his finest three-word truism is "It's all relative." Plus, it aligns so well with this chapter. Stay with me.

What do Snowflakes value?

Respect.

What do they abhor?

Perceived disrespect.

Now go find a grove of Cacti and inquire about their top values. Respect will make an entrance on the short list. And what can they not abide? Perceived disrespect. Same stuff.

What's going on? We've been mulling over the vast variances between Snowflakes and Cacti. How can they share values and pet peeves? And why am I throwing around the word "perceived"?

All your fine questions will be answered. Yet first we'll indulge in a very compact worksheet.

WORKSHEET: Find Out What It Means to Me

Define respect.

Really think it over. I'll wait.

Respect=_____

_____

_____

Tap, tap, tap. Not so easy, is it? Do your best.

Webster's Dictionary correlates respect with consideration. Be courteous, polite, civil.

Hold it right there. What's the crux of the matter? Respect is not a simple construct. While theoretically respect is a widely shared value, its embodiments can be like night and day. Respect is demonstrated in profoundly different ways among Snowflakes and Cacti.

Plus, we have nuanced versions of experiencing respect. Suddenly a basic concept starts to resemble a bowl of tangled spaghetti. Perception is the sauce.

What is the knee-jerk response to being respectful? Treat others how I like to be treated. Sound familiar? To dredge up old memories, I paraphrased the Golden Rule. Treating others how you want to be treated is woven into the fabric of guidelines for positive living across the world.

Now for the blasphemy. I tossed out the ubiquitous Golden Rule years ago.

Infused with good intentions, this principle frequently comes up short. For example, the way I demonstrate respect may have little in common with your preferences.

Does a + b = c ?

If (a) I believe others demonstrate respect by greeting me as I pass by . . .

And (b) I greet those I walk past, including you . . .

Does it follow that (c) You feel respected by me?

Not necessarily. What works for a Snowflake can fall flat for a Cactus. While Snowflakes may feel revved up by morning salutations, Cacti might feel annoyed or drained.

Suddenly $a+b \neq c$

What a mess. What are we to do now? Enter . . .

THE PLATINUM RULE

The Golden Rule is so 2008. Let bygones be bygones and retire it on a dusty top shelf. Join me in upgrading to the bright and glistening Platinum Rule. Infinitely more malleable, the Platinum Rule entreats that we:

Treat others how *they* want to be treated.

The Platinum Rule is a game changer.

Snip-snap, I predict daily interactions will play out quite differently than in the past. Your new strategies for interactions will often differ from your standard penchants.

Implementation requires paying attention to others' preferences. It takes practice. The effort pays off. Test-drive the Platinum Rule and let me know what you think. And how you feel.

Following the Platinum Rule means aligning your focus with others' core concerns. It does not require a cosmic internal shift. Come hop aboard.

THE RUBBER HITS THE ROAD
The "Care About You" Collision

Beth is a Snowflake. Her colleague, Allison, is a Cactus. They've worked together for several years, not without conflict. One day Allison shows up to a meeting looking a bit off. Most people wouldn't notice, yet Beth prides herself on picking up subtle shifts in energy.

Beth pulls Allison aside and queries, "Hey, Ally, you okay?"

Allison is uncomfortable and stiffly replies, "What? Yeah, I'm fine." She is not about to discuss her emotions at work.

Sensing an issue bubbling below the surface, Beth persists. "You can tell me. We've worked together forever. I care, and you seem upset. What's up?"

Allison glares at her and walks out of the room.

Hit the pause button.

Beth is behaving the way she'd want Allison to react if Beth came to work out of sorts. This tactic is not working for Allison—at all. Beth's effort to build rapport with Allison is an epic backfire. Despite earnest intentions, their relationship is unraveling faster than a novice knitter's first scarf. Quick! Someone parachute down reminders of the Platinum Rule.

Beth is making Allison uncomfortable, annoyed, and irritated by the unwelcome intrusion. Allison makes a mental note to further distance herself.

As a side note, Beth can forget about Allison ever behaving this way toward her. It won't happen. Allison believes in giving others their space and staying out of their business. A few weeks later, when Beth shows up visibly weary and battling a cold, it doesn't occur to Allison to say a word. Before Beth reads this book, she is upset and hurt.

After reading this book, she knows it's nothing personal and reminds herself to maintain realistic expectations of others. Setting aside her own partialities, Beth would have stopped after, "Hey, Ally, you okay?" That would be a more effective demonstration of respect to her Cactus coworker.

And Allison, if she's up to it, might venture a "Hope you feel better quick," in response to Beth's announcement that she's under the weather.

Disposition explains preferences while placing zero limitations on your possible range of behaviors. How you live in the world is up to you and your choices. Just keep accumulating a variety of skills and a wide range of adaptive behaviors.

I think you're really going to like this next technique. It's called:

Flexing Your Style

Flexing your style means adapting to others' modus operandi. There are three requirements:

- Comprehension of your natural style

- Awareness of others' preferred modes of communication

- Flexibility to adapt your behaviors to best fit the situation

    Takes a bit of discipline up front.

Why bother? Well, for starters it's a surefire way to improve rapport, build coalitions, motivate, and create common ground. As a side benefit, it is impossible to zone out while flexing.

Learned Behaviors ≠ Innate Preferences

Be assured: Adopting useful traits from the other side of the tracks does not change who you are. I am frequently asked, "If I shift my reactions to workplace demands, does that mean I will occupy a more middle position on the spectrum?" My answer is *no*. Flexing your style means expanding the range of your responses. It does not alter your essence one iota. We need you as you are. Some flexibility thrown into the mix just adds options and vibrancy.

Why You?

It's easy to fall into the trap of "Why should I be the one to adapt?" To which I reply, "Why not?" Most people don't have the awareness or ability to flex their style. It's a fantastic skill to harness; why not own it?

It's not about who is more senior. It's not about how things *should* be. It's not about who's right or wrong. It is about what matters to you. Being right? Pride? Holding your ground? What resonates in your core? Keep your eye on the prize.

Flexing definitely comes in particularly handy when people are on different wavelengths.

THE RUBBER HITS THE ROAD
Bottom Line

A national nonprofit was preparing for its annual gala. The upscale event is regarded as their top fundraiser of the year, featuring, among other things, a live auction.

A few weeks prior to the big night, a major donor, Delusha, stopped by the executive director's office unannounced. She asked for a few moments of his time. Once seated, she launched into the purpose of her visit. "As you know, I've attended the gala year after year and always throw my full support into our mission." The director, Joe, quickly agreed and offered her a small bag of organic dried fruit and locally sourced water. Delusha, a board member and active volunteer, merited his full attention.

"Honestly, this has bothered me for years. I can't stand it when the auction caller shouts out the donation amounts. This isn't about money; it's about the future of our planet. Usually, I walk out during the auction. Can't we make it private, with the bidders whispering pledges to our senior vice president of finances?"

Delusha took a sip of water and continued, "Someone with limited financial means might feel bad they are donating at a lower level. Doesn't that fly in the face of our values statement to treat everyone respectfully? Nothing is more important than that!" Even as a Snowflake, she was aggravated by her tears welling up. She hastily wiped her eyes with a tissue, hoping to disguise her encroaching emotions.

Variations on this topic had been on Joe's radar for as long as he could remember. A Cactus surrounded by Snowflakes, he recognized the auction format pitted feelings against monetary and programmatic results. The organization relied heavily on charitable donations. As a nonprofit professional for nearly thirty years, he knew the drill—members give more when the donation is made public.

This isn't about humility or righteousness; it is about fundraising ran through his head. Yet he knew responding from a Cactus perspective would alienate Delusha. Instead, he replied, "I appreciate how deeply you care about this. There are so many ways we benefit from your sensitivity to others. I wonder if we can bridge the gap somehow. I know we both want our organization to be around for a long time!"

Notice he did not say or imply her perspective was wrong. Nor did he express explicit agreement. Instead, he directed their attention toward shared desired outcomes.

Working from this common ground, Delusha and Joe decided to offer a silent auction along with the traditional live auction at the gala. Both components won rave reviews and record-breaking revenue.

I Agree

An impasse in conversation is often due to conflicting viewpoints. I want this, you want that, so one of us will be despondent. If instead we focus on mutual interests, that's a whole other ballgame.

Few two-word combinations are more powerful than "I agree." Plus, genuine agreement is more accessible than is often recognized. In the preceding scenario, Delusha and Joe moved forward by identifying what they agreed upon, such as shared values, a successful event, and achieving the organization's mission. When faced with differing perspectives, be on the lookout for shared values.

As you've seen, flexing is quite useful when engaging with others. Up next is another way flexing one's style can amp up effectiveness.

THE RUBBER HITS THE ROAD
Will the Real You Please Stand Up?

Enter Anthony, a seasoned senior executive at a multinational conglomerate. He's a straight shooter, not holding back when disagreeing about a new product strategy. His tough exterior is well known. In other words, a prototypical Cactus. Or is he? Let's take a closer look.

"Feel" is scattered throughout his conversation like sprinkles on an ice cream cone. Anthony is sentimental and fiercely loyal. He's the first to sign up for volunteer committees, and when off the clock, his texts to friends are strewn with emojis. He gets misty-eyed over corny movies. What is going on here?

Anthony is a Flaker. His *learned behavior* for certain circumstances is Cactus. Is Anthony authentic? Indubitably. Long ago he recognized the value of flexing his style. He earned his success through an unflinching commitment to his workplace. His behavior reflects how deeply he cares about his coworkers and outcomes. He demonstrates unwavering respect through his actions: giving others his full attention, recognizing varied perspectives, and offering assistance in areas of professional development.

MINDING YOUR OWN BUSINESS

One often overlooked component of respecting others is staying out of their business.

We can be such know-it-alls! We think we know what's going on in others' heads as well as what is best—or worst— for them. Inventive busybodies, we can lose ourselves in making up stories about others.

Living in other people's business is lazy. When loitering around your business, I don't do anything but get in the way. When I'm in my own business I've got to get to it! There's a lot to tidy up in there.

A particularly foolhardy intrusion is pretending I know what you think about me. I'll offer up an old standard: *She doesn't like me.*

I can neither prove nor disprove this. It might be true. Then again, it might not. I may never be entirely certain. We can play around with that belief, though, and explore alternatives. There are several ways to turn my perception around; all it takes is some dexterity with reframing.* That the turnarounds may not be factual can be a thorn in the

*Reframing entails altering our perspective. More on this in chapter 4.

side of a Cactus. Then again, they might ring as true or truer than the original statement. Let's try these on for size:

1. *I* don't like *her*.
2. She *does* like me.
3. *I* don't like me.
4. She's not thinking about me.

Number one. Let's consider the first switch-a-rooney. I've noticed when I think someone doesn't like me, the reverse is nearly always the case. Do you concur?

Number two is the most upbeat and has plenty of potential to jump-start a shift in our dynamics. What if I suddenly decided that she *does* like me? How differently would I engage with her? How would it influence our interactions?

Number three is a tough pill to swallow. Yet we're better off addressing our own self-esteem issues than passing our days reflecting on whether others like us.

Hold on to your hat for number four. That last one entertains the possibility that whatever's going on isn't about me at all. Have you ever had an exchange that sent your head into a tailspin because of a perceived snub, stab, or slight? Then you're later privy to information revealing that what transpired actually had nothing at all to do with you?

Imagine other occasions that left you upset, confused, or offended, although you never had the opportunity to discover whether it was all due to misinterpretation. Next time you head down this path, I offer up a sage acronym for your use:

NAY

What does NAY stand for, pray tell? Not About You. Next time you are precariously close to succumbing to the whirling dark hole of attributing intent, say NAY!

What's a pathway to more positive (Snowflake driver) and productive (Cactus driver) interactions? Replace speculation about others' mind-sets with consciously resetting your own.

I heard a senior executive speak at his retirement event. He shared some of the biggest lessons learned over the course of an illustrious career. One observation really stuck with me:

**If you think you know everything
about a situation, you're wrong.**

Over several decades, he dealt with many touchy situations where everyone had an opinion. He knew none of those steadfast judgments were based on knowledge of the big picture. The more certain you are, the better idea it is to take a step back.

RESERVE JUDGMENT

Iconic rock band Van Halen entered the music world in the 1970s. They proceeded to dominate the hard rock scene for decades, led by front man David Lee Roth. Reports emerged about a clause in their venue contracts demanding that a mandatory backstage bowl of M&Ms would include no brown ones. This stipulation was buried deep within a complex rider addressing sound, lighting, safety, and other critical protocols for their concerts.

At first glance, requiring a vendor to hand-sort the candies seems absurd. Furthermore, finding a single brown candy was grounds for dismissal. How could this possibly be justifiable?

Upon learning of this contract proviso, a Snowflake might deem it unfair. A Cactus might critique the specification as illogical. Yet either's assumptions will shift once they are privy to full information—and grasp the eclipsed *Why?* behind the demand.

The band later explained they slipped that clause deep into the contract to ensure the promoter read every word, not overlooking other requirements that were critical for a safe, positive concert experience.

BOY, YOU BLEW IT!

When you're in a position to give advice, watch out when it is unsolicited. Clarify why you are compelled to offer your two cents.

There are plenty of cases when offering input or assistance is a magnanimous gesture. Yet in certain circumstances, so-called advice is far from benevolent. Fortunately, there is a litmus test. It comes in the form of a question to ask yourself: *Is it too late?* Let's say you believe someone made an error in judgment yet already proceeded. Perhaps it was a relocation, major purchase, elective surgery, or email sent.

Reiterating that a poor choice was made or how badly they blew it does nothing to improve the situation. The best thing you can do is listen and provide support moving forward. That's respectful.

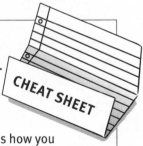

- Practice the Platinum Rule: Treat others how they want to be treated.
- Flex your style to meet others where they're at.
- Focus on your own business. That's how you can make the biggest splash.

CHAPTER FOUR

The Nonevent

ALTERNATIVE REALITIES & BEANS UP THE NOSE

And those who were seen dancing were thought insane by those who could not hear the music.

—FRIEDRICH NIETZSCHE

POP QUIZ!
WHAT IF A TREE FALLS?

Q: If a tree falls in a forest, causing one person to feel sad and another to merely stroll along, who's right?

A: Talk about a philosophical dilemma! There is no single answer.

What happens when nothing turns out to be something? Or when something is considered nothing? Introducing . . .

THE NONEVENT

I cannot overstate my excitement over introducing this concept. I hope within a few pages you'll unite with me in singing its praises. Anything to drown out my off-key efforts.

When understood, the nonevent revolutionizes relationships. When ignored, it yields cosmic strife. We shall hereafter refer to nonevents as NE.

Conflict is not inherently rooted in difference of opinions. Frequently it stems from underlying gaps of perception. A disconnect in the experience of reality itself.

The Spectacle of Alternative Realities

Perhaps you've experienced the NE phenomenon firsthand. Here's one way an NE may play out.

You're a Snowflake and have a powerful experience, positive or negative. You may even deem it a defining moment. You turn to a nearby Cactus to process.

The Cactus, who was right there next to you when it happened, has no idea what you're talking about. It's not a matter of spacing out. It's that in the Cactus's realm nothing occurred!

Supreme Wind Gusts

Let's say it is a chilly, blustery day with wind gusts up to 30 mph [48 kph]. While no hurricane, this degree of wind still significantly impacts a real-life snowflake. From a Snowflaker's perspective, the entire arc of the day shifts from a peaceful downward drift into a whirling, chaotic trajectory. By nightfall the snowflake is exhausted.

Now let's whiz over to the cactus habitat, where there are equally strong winds. A cactus doesn't even notice; there is zero impact on its day. To the standard cactus, a moderate wind is an NE.

Snowflake = Major event.
Cactus = Nothing happened.

Why is this momentous? Because if privy to a snowflake's reaction to wind, the cactus would classify it as an overreaction.

I beseech you, from this page forward, to resist judging others' reactions. Deviating experiences of the same objective reality are labeled as inaccurate, short-sighted, absurd. What is actually the case? More often than not, metaphorical Snowflakes and Cacti have contradictory experiences of identical events. To the untrained eye, one reaction is faulty.

Next time someone responds to a stimulus in a manner that is inexplicable to you, test out this useful rule of thumb:

Resist comparing my insides with others' outsides.

If an event has no effect on me while propelling you into a downward spiral, I may classify your reaction as overly dramatic. This could lead me to say, "You shouldn't feel that way." Now the hurt you felt from our original interaction is compounded by my cavalier comment. I'm devaluing your experience. This wreaks havoc on relationships.

NEs go both ways. Nobody gets a pass.

A noteworthy experience to me is potentially an NE to others:

- A neighbor passes me by and doesn't greet me.

- A coworker ignores me in an elevator.

- A family member has no reaction when I share a dramatic news story.

Likewise, a significant experience for someone else can be an NE to me:

- A friend makes an apparently off-handed remark, and I do not reply.

- A colleague belatedly joins a meeting, which I do not notice so do not greet them.

- A coworker is triggered by raised voices that do not register with me.

ENTER THE META-STATE

Let's give a warm welcome to the meta-state! (Halfhearted, scattered applause accompanied by tiptoeing to the lukewarm coffee.)

The concept of a meta-state can appear a bit esoteric at first glance. A brief definition is the first step toward clearing up any brain haze:

**Meta-states are our inner reactions
to primary thoughts and feelings.**

An initial response to an event is called a primary state. "I am disappointed" is an example of a primary state reaction.

The meta-state occurs at a higher, more conscious level. It is a state in reference to the first state, often based in curiosity and geared toward a higher understanding. Such as:

- "I notice I felt angry."

- "I had a visceral aversion to his comment."

- "I wonder why I felt so disappointed."

Meta-states are valuable because they create an opportunity to reflect upon ourselves and our experiences, shifting and shaping future reactions.

NEURO-LINGUISTIC PROGRAMMING

Our exploration of meta-states draws on a methodology introduced in Neuro-Linguistic Programming (NLP). As a certified practitioner of this cognitive science, I've sprinkled several applications based on NLP throughout this volume. In a nutshell, NLP features a variety of systems that improve the way we build rapport and engage in the world. It also fine-tunes our conscious use of linguistic and kinesthetic communication.

I gather this can sound a bit heady.

I'm just providing a smidgen of background and moving along. Like sneaking a few veggies into your tuna casserole. You'll hardly notice the extra perk.

Reframing Reactions

Entering a meta-state can also reconfigure our perceptions of others.

Perhaps your reaction to an event makes no sense to me. My primary state is irritation. However, I insert a micro-pause, giving myself time to engage in a meta-state. I may think to myself, *Hmm, I saw Ari got really upset at that meeting. We seem to have had opposite experiences of the same encounter. I wonder how I can be helpful in finding common ground.*

I've removed my initial judgment and accompanying frustration. I'm curious rather than annoyed. In the process, tension is released.

THE RUBBER HITS THE ROAD

"Sure!"

Ian, an exceedingly upset Snowflake client, phoned me. He was at the end of his rope with a Cactus collaborator. Ian warned me this was a potentially unsavable situation. He had been feeling repeatedly disrespected and belittled. I asked for details.

"I'll give you a recent example. Keep in mind this kind of thing happens *all the time!* I spent half my weekend composing a carefully worded email to my colleague requesting that he join our department's efforts to craft a major grant proposal. I sent it at 9:30 am Monday morning. Within minutes he replied: 'Sure.'"

Ian paused for my reaction.

Between you and me, I had no idea what was happening. I awaited his next statement.

"I can't believe how dismissive he was," Ian concluded. "Of course, it would have been completely different if he had written 'Sure!' with an exclamation mark."

I kid you not. I was quickly losing track of the situation. "Wait, he *agreed* to your request, right? And he did so rather quickly?"

"Well, yes," Ian reluctantly acknowledged. "But he didn't put any time or energy into his email. It felt flippant."

I ventured this could merely be his colleague's method to crank through emails on a Monday morning. I felt certain this entire exchange had been an NE on the other side of the coin. Yet I knew simply telling Ian to forget about it would not be enough in this case. It happened they had a meeting scheduled later in the day regarding another matter. We decided Ian would take a moment to calmly mention his reaction to the "Sure," opening the door for his colleague to respond.

Ian reported back that the conversation was a success, and he doubted he would duplicate his inner reaction to a "Sure" in the future—with or without the exclamation mark.

Bear in mind our continual interest in understanding rather than modifying others.

The intended outcome of the preceding situation was not to change his colleague's personality. Ian's objective was to dissipate the tension via clear, open communication.

TOOLSHED MOMENT
A Ruler

This is an elegant tool for the next time you freak out (a highly technical term). Imagine you are beside yourself over an altercation with a coworker. Incensed, you cannot stop mulling over the injustice incurred. Here's where I step in, cape swinging in the breeze. I hand you a classic foot-long wooden ruler (unless you prefer metrics, to which I would readily adapt). Keep it handy. Next time you find yourself getting worked up over an untoward situation, pull out your ruler. Better yet, situate it prominently for continual use.

PART ONE:
Ask yourself, *On a scale of one to twelve inches, how significant is this current circumstance in the big picture?* One inch = inconsequential. Twelve inches = cosmic implosion.

Point to the place on the ruler where today's situation seems to belong. I predict you will see a trend of very few incidents meriting a spot past a couple of inches.

PART TWO:

Ask yourself, *How likely is it I will recall this situation even occurred one year from now?* I venture to guess the response you give the vast majority of the time is, *Extremely unlikely.*

POP QUIZ!
SYMBOLIC VERSUS PRACTICAL

A Snowflake obtains a complimentary T-shirt at a long-anticipated footrace. Unfortunately, his participation does not pan out as hoped. Two-thirds of the way through, a misstep on a curb brings him down. A badly twisted ankle lands him in a boot for ten weeks rather than in the winner's circle as he'd visualized.

Question #1 Does the Snowflake ever wear the shirt again?

Your response (include why): _____

_____

Question #2 Would a Cactus ever wear the shirt again?

Your response (include why): _____

_____

ANSWER #1
Snowflake: "Never again. That shirt is infused with bad karma and bad memories. It got tossed into my donation pile faster than you could say "#*&$@%!'"

ANSWER #2
Cactus: "Absolutely. That question seems like a non sequitur. The shirt was free, it's clean, and it fits. Throw it on."

The symbolism of the shirt's origin to a Snowflake is an NE to the Cactus.

The NE concept is nothing if not versatile. Even a humble ruler can be your trusty assistant in making an inner shift, involving no outside parties.

Utilizing this visceral reminder alongside a dollop of perspective, you can transform an apparent big deal into an NE, fizzling out faster than a discount store sparkler.

CONVERSATION OR CONFLICT

Are Flakers conflict avoidant? Life is more intricate than that. Snowflakes *perceive* conflict differently than Cacti. It's like observing "This wine seems to be red" at an upscale tasting. You're hovering at the first level of a sophisticated analysis.

Say that a pair of colleagues are catching up on the phone. As their planned agenda winds down, the Cactus changes gears and asks her coworker his opinion about a hotly contested political issue. When he tentatively responds, she plays devil's advocate, challenging his point of view. The conversation wraps up within moments.

What happened from the Snowflake's point of view? Somehow the phone call devolved into a distressing altercation that left him reeling. Why were they arguing? That night he can't sleep, going over and over the argument in his head and wondering how to mend the relationship. He perceived—indeed, experienced—an upsetting and unexpected confrontation.

Let's travel to the desert and see how the Cactus is doing. She is in high spirits. Working from home has left her craving nonwork-related interactions. A spirited debate with her colleague was precisely the pick-me-up she needed to relieve stress. She is grateful for the stimulating discussion and pours herself a glass of that wine that seems to be red. The presumed confrontation? An NE from this Cactus's garden.

The basic inquiry is not whether Snowflakes avoid conflict due to experiencing discomfort. The real starting point is defining what we classify as conflict. The previous scenario was regarded as an argument by the Snowflake and a pick-me-up by the Cactus. The encounter had a negative impact on the former and a positive one on the latter.

A casual conversation to one transforms into a competition or clash to another. It's a slippery slope.

HAZARD ALERT: ALTERCATION!

Cacti get a kick out of—even crave—what they deem friendly competition. To a Snowflake that sounds like an oxymoron. Who would string together the words *friendly* and *competition*? The word *competition* raises the adrenaline level of both temperaments for entirely divergent reasons. Cacti get revved up in a positive way. Snowflakes feel the blood coursing in a fight-or-flight sort of way. Danger ahead!

While affable sparring generally energizes a Cactus, the same interaction provokes anxiety in a Snowflake. And guess what? Neither reaction is flawed whatsoever.

How Could I Have Been So Rude?

The other day I spoke with a colleague who happens to be a Cactus. You're correct, by now it was a number of days ago.

Without thinking, I made a careless remark that could easily be interpreted as an insult. Our next meeting was scheduled for the following week, and there was no opportunity to speak beforehand. For seven days, I lamented my inexcusably rude inference, certain our relationship was permanently scarred. Internal debates raged in my mind as I grappled with the best approach for when we next spoke.

My fretting was to no avail. She joined the call in her usual jocular manner, greeting me with enthusiasm. My remark had been a quintessential NE from her stance.

Alongside my relief, I recognized a twinge of envy. How marvelous to let potential slights effortlessly slide away, perhaps never even noticing them. Admittedly, when the shoe is on the other foot I am not naturally as resilient.

I told a Cactus about how this situation unfolded. She added her own insight: that labeling a discourse as "insensitive of me" depends largely on who's with me. Good point.

Then I relayed this Cactus's comment to a Snowflake, who responded that erring on the side of caution when it comes to making insensitive remarks is better than being careless. She surmised that "no one would be offended that someone apologizes to them."

I ran this by a Cactus, who clarified that while she'd be unlikely to take offense, it's quite likely she'd be irritated by continual or needless apologizing. She advised that Snowflakes simply refrain from "losing sleep or peace of mind worrying about whether or not they were insensitive." I needn't poll a crowd of Snowflakes to know this well-meaning advice is easier said than done.

And so it goes, a seesaw of personality perceptions.

HAZARD ALERT: ACHILLES' HEELS!

Most everyone has an Achilles' heel or two.* Some variances are rooted in temperament. They're often subconscious, increasing the potential hazard. As a humble attempt at community service, we'll dredge up common examples for each nuanced nature.

Guilt: A Snowflake's Dilemma

Like it or not, guilt is a defining characteristic of most Snowflakes. It's not all shimmering crystals. Snowflakes can obsess over guilt. At times they are paralyzed with guilt, hindering their ability to go about their day. It can be rooted in a situation or free-floating, without a clear origin.

In other instances, Snowflakes can—we may as well admit it!—erroneously attribute their guilt to unsuspecting external sources. Occasionally a Snowflake will unceremoniously toss a bucket of guilt across a conference room.

Guilt is the Snowflake's Achilles' heel.

THE RUBBER HITS THE ROAD

Book It!

A Snowflake book editor, Noah, confided to me the following experience. He was invited to attend a high-level publishing meeting with many heavy hitters from the industry. Participants were asked to plan on sharing a recurring challenge for the group to discuss and troubleshoot.

---

* A weakness amid overall strength, based on Achilles of Greek mythology.

Noah was raring to go, looking forward to receiving advice on the following problem:

"I often find that authors hate their book covers. It happens a lot and is very upsetting. What do you recommend?"

A silence filled the room as the seasoned professionals displayed looks of pure confusion. They evidently didn't grasp the issue. Finally, one blurted out what seemed to be coursing through everyone's mind: "Get over it!"

The same happens to Cacti editors on the reg . . . it's simply not considered a problem.

NE! That's life.

Tone: A Cactus Conundrum

Cacti don't give a lot of thought to the concept of tone. Many think it's ridiculous that anyone would. Communication is cut and dried, like shrink-wrapped beef jerky without the optional teriyaki. An accusatory tone, off-putting to some, can be a classic NE to more prickly types. A Cactus's overlooked nuance could propel a Snowflake to suddenly— and inexplicably to the Cactus—withdraw from a potential collaboration.

Snowflakes give as much credence to how we speak as the words themselves. Tone can make or break the conversation. Consider the inquiry "What do you want?" Spoken gently, with a slight lilt, it indicates compassionate interest. Spoken gruffly, with a scowl and emphasis on "you," it sends a message of annoyed aggravation. Yet many Cacti would either not notice the variance or give no credence to the fluctuation.

Tone encroaches into written communication as well. This gets even more dicey, as we tend to layer our own "voice" onto others' words. How do we really know the intended—or even unintended—tones of written communication? On the one hand, we do not, unless especially well acquainted with another person. On the other hand, sometimes tone seemingly leaps out from the page or screen. Adding to the chaos, there's a strong likelihood that the aforementioned leaping tone can be interpreted in entirely different ways.

Time for another edifying example.

THE RUBBER HITS THE ROAD
Knockin' on Your Door

Miriam recently began working from home. She was in charge of securing permits for an upcoming event and submitted the necessary forms two months ahead of time. Because she had not heard back and the deadline was imminent, she emailed her point of contact, whom she had never met, to inquire about the status. "When should we expect to receive our permits? I filed the paperwork in October. Thanks!" she wrote.

The response came that very afternoon, yet it was not a reply she had anticipated.

"I have been to your house personally twice over the last month, attempting to deliver your permits. There has been no answer at the door. —Gary"

Miriam was stunned. New to the teleworking model, she was acutely aware of differences from working at headquarters. Stopping by security at the front desk of an office building is one thing; appearing unannounced at a stranger's personal residence is another altogether. Did this guy actually think she would open the door?

In Miriam's opinion, Gary conveyed as cryptic and rather punitive. He was almost certainly a Cactus, like herself. She ran the situation by her neighbor James, who provided an alternative interpretation. James suggested that from Gary's point of view he was going above and beyond, taking it upon himself to hand deliver the documentation. James mused that both parties could benefit from informal collaborative interpreters, regardless of heralding from the same side of the tracks.

Postscript: Miriam and Gary met in person a few months later at a corporate event. Unlike in their written communication, they had immediate rapport and became allies. Miriam discovered that James's insight was spot on; it turned out Gary did epitomize the concept of going the extra mile. There's something to be said for meeting face to face.

Internalizing and Projecting

A psychological concept relevant to NEs is called *internalizing*. We'll work from a basic definition.

INTERNALIZING: Incorporating within oneself others' values, culture, habits, and inner frameworks.

Snowflakes are prone to assuming others' emotional states. Envision a placid Snowflake entering a meeting where a colleague is highly agitated. If the Snowflake soon becomes equally worked up, taking on the other's mood, that is an example of internalizing.

Albeit sometimes we make something out of nothing. This is a particular stumbling block for highly emotive Snowflakes, who might imagine another's presumed agita.

Consider the following. Dafne shows up at work appearing demoralized. Her coworker Glen finds himself becoming despondent. He begins to internalize Dafne's presumed mood. Yet what if Glen misread the situation? Perhaps Dafne entered while lost in thought over a poignant article she read the previous evening. Glen's reaction could have been based on an NE. He was internalizing his own perception.

Projecting incurs a similar hazard. This multidimensional notion can be succinctly described as follows.

PROJECTING: Placing one's feelings or concerns onto another person.

I'll offer an explanation by way of example, provided by Barb in Information Technology.

Barb was insecure in her new job requiring extensive technical expertise. She quietly questioned whether she was even qualified for the position. At project meetings, she frequently felt dismissed when making suggestions. She began accusing others of rejecting her input out of hand. Her teammates denied this, insisting they had only admiration for her subject matter knowledge. Yet Barb pinned her self-doubt onto those around her, spinning NEs into all-out brawls.

As you go about your day, be open to the possibility you may be internalizing or projecting, inadvertently creating NEs. Snowflakes, in particular, take heed. Reality checks are your friends.

And now one more angle on NEs. A peerless guideline to subvert endless headaches.

BEANS UP THE NOSE

Beans up the Nose is a memorable metaphor for how we can unwittingly sabotage ourselves by creating a mess out of what began as an NE.

Here's the scenario. You're a grade school teacher embarking on a highly anticipated dried bean art project with your class. It features white glue, a sturdy canvas, and an array of colorful dried beans to glue to the canvas. It begins well, with your little artists fully engaged, creating singular patterns and imagery. Then you have a crucial lapse in judgment. As an afterthought, you cheerfully caution, "Now class, don't put beans up your nose." Jolted out of their reverie, the students can now only think of one thing.

Beans start going up noses.

Any of us can make a comparable mistake. Imagine you're about to clinch an informational interview with a sought-after advertising firm. You offhandedly toss out, "I can't wait to meet up with you, especially after tanking at my meeting with [arch-rival company] last week."

Or you're about to enter a second round of interviews as a communications director and this flies out of your mouth: "Of course, not much of what I've done in the past translates to a virtual environment—I'm always messing up our WebEx meetings."

How about, "I spilled orange juice on the top I originally planned to wear on this video call. The replacement I have on is pretty ratty. Please ignore it."

Are you drawing others' attention toward something that might never have entered their minds? Are you impairing your own success?

Take control of the situation. Restrain yourself from:

- Pointing out what could go wrong
- Provoking others to reconsider
- Offering examples of your shortcomings
- Saying what not to do

I beg you! Prescreen all slapdash statements with the inner query *Is this beans up the nose?*

In short, do not suggest things to suggestible people.

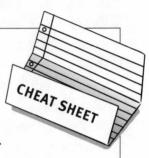

- A powerful experience for one can simultaneously be a *nonevent* (NE) to another.

- Meta-states can help illuminate and refine our primary responses.

- Refrain from letting those beans go up noses.

CHAPTER FIVE

Thoughts, Words, Actions

THE THREE AREAS YOU CONTROL

Stop letting people who do so little for you control so much of your mind, feelings, and emotions.

—WILL SMITH

You are, no doubt, overflowing with brilliant ideas for how others could improve their functioning. After all, much of what goes on out there is inexplicably incompetent.

We expend sooo much energy correcting others within our own minds. It's as fruitless as pouring a newly frothed latte down the drain. Ain't gonna wake you up.

Focus your attention on fine-tuning yourself rather than futilely attempting to fix others, change the barometric pressure, or alter reality. I've got news for you, sugarplum. You're off the hook. Because there are precisely three things you control: your own thoughts, your own words, and your own actions. That's it.

Thoughts, Words, Actions = TWA

From this day forward you're freed up. You can keep your nose out of what is beyond your control. Which is nearly everything. What a relief! Your to-do list got a lot more manageable.

Know what drives me nuts? Besides being served soggy french fries? Those heady T-shirts and posters that proclaim, "You can do anything! Just apply your mind [for Cacti] or heart [for Snowflakes]." The reality is, most of us cannot do *many*, if not *most* things.

I don't mean to be a buzzkill. Au contraire. This little revelation can be elevating. Let's brainstorm. Among the sundry matters you cannot control are yesterday and tomorrow. The past, in particular, is wildly beyond our realm of influence, yet we spend a crushing amount of time dwelling there.

The main thing you *can* do is be your full self. That'll keep you busy and productive for a lifetime. So, let's redirect, shall we? A thorough coordination of TWA can alter routines, enhance well-being, and improve relationships.

Release expectations that others will master their TWA. Most people are not that evolved. Let it go. Life is more satisfying when we focus on what we can control vs. what we cannot.

THOUGHTS

Our journey to the inner world begins with life filters. They can be courtesy of embedded thought patterns, deeply entrenched memories, or recent developments.

Short-term, transient filters can include:

- Enjoying an unexpectedly fabulous day
- Hearing from a long-lost friend
- Feeling under the weather

- Overcooking dinner
- Running out of gas (literally or figuratively)

Deeply rooted filters can include:

- Childhood memories
- Past trauma
- Successful experiences
- Significant life moments
- Defining relationships

Long-term filters can also stem from learned beliefs such as:

- I'm a worthy person.
- You can't trust anyone.
- There's always someone to blame.
- Mistakes can be avoided.
- People mean well.

Whether short- or long-term, filters influence the ebb and flow of our thoughts. Cacti are more likely to put a pragmatic spin on experiences, whereas Snowflakes seek layers of meaning. Either way, complete control of our thoughts is nearly impossible.

Some self-proclaimed spiritual gurus say they can empty their mind of thoughts. However, the rest of us don't fall into that category of humans. It's kind of like how Hollywood features flawless human specimens, leading the other 99.9999 percent of the human race to feel inadequate. Okay, I didn't conduct a statistical analysis; I kinda leaned on the 9 key.

While Zen retreats and mind-body-spirit centers proclaim the obtainability of controlling your mind, most of us—with our full-time jobs, domestic responsibilities, and demanding relatives—may want to start with a lower bar. We'll call it *thought supervision*. It's still worthwhile. Kinda like being a fine home cook while cutting a few recipe-step corners. (I'm fairly certain "fresh herbs" means the jar's expiration date is a few weeks out.)

What can we run-of-the-mill mortals do? Keep reading.

Self-Talk

Self-talk is how we communicate with ourselves. Mostly silently, although who am I to judge if I inadvertently overhear audible mumbling? Some thoughts are directed outward—on matters beyond our control. Others are directed inward—on our individual thoughts, words, and actions.

Think of self-talk as an internal audio loop, similar to an inner monologue. If transcribed into written form, the text would be your thoughts; the motivation propelling the thoughts onward is the subtext. At times self-talk is negative, focusing on what's wrong. Other self-talk is positive, such as applauding a job well done.

Here's what doesn't work: *I oughtn't have thought that.* How is that helpful? The fact of the matter is, you *did*. What, now you're going to beat up on yourself for a thought that already occurred? Sounds like the definition of futile.

Instead, addressing self-talk entails peaceably recognizing, *Look, I had this thought in response to an occurrence. How could I rewrite my response?* There's a system, rooted in learning to recognize, accept, and revise our thoughts. Think of it as mental calisthenics.

TOOLSHED MOMENT
Recognize, Accept, and Revise

Welcome to our *Recognize, Accept, Revise (RAR) Model*, offering a soothing alternative to haranguing yourself for falling short of perfection. Here's how the system works:

STEP ONE: *Recognize* the emergence of a thought that does not serve you well.

STEP TWO: Without judgment, *accept* that you had this thought.

STEP THREE: *Revise* the initial thought with a new and improved alternative. Consider thoughts that will better serve you rather than continually looping backward.

RAR works for either style. Flakers are more apt to succumb to harmful thoughts. Cacti disassociate from thought patterns more easily than their tender-hearted counterparts, although this practical, systematic model resonates with their nature. Both have much to gain from implementing this system.

Next time you notice yourself in a negative self-talk pattern, test-drive the RAR model. And while implementing any of the tools offered up throughout this section, remember:

Thoughts ≠ Facts

Thoughts are a big deal. We grow accustomed to our version of thinking. We get increasingly attached to our belief patterns, until response systems become nearly automated. Yet thoughts are not inherently true or accurate.

Self-talk and the RAR construct are inner-directed, aiming to address and alleviate internal struggles. *Thought supervision* can also assist in external situations. Coming up is an example of how a shift in perception can alter and improve relationships.

THE RUBBER HITS THE ROAD
Just Eduardo

Let's face it, people can be vexing.

Naomi, a Snowflake senior executive in the transportation industry, was continually flummoxed by the Cactus CEO, Eduardo. He habitually made comments that rubbed her the wrong way, yet clearly valued her contributions. Cognitively, she knew he meant no offense, yet she found herself mulling over their conversations well into her off-hours.

Then she had a revelation. It made all the difference and did not require anyone to magically acquire a new personality. Naomi began to substitute her visceral reactions with the simple inner reminder *It's just Eduardo.*

That was all. She began to invoke a reminder to herself, *It's just his way.* The impact was immediate. Plus, she stopped telling herself stories about his behavior. By shifting her thought patterns, she could cheerfully disengage. No more internalization or aggravation.

Like Naomi, you are also well on the pathway toward successfully supervising your thoughts.

Focus on What You *Can* Do

Entreating others to "not let their thoughts take over" is a naïve campaign, because as neuroscientists well know:

Our brains cannot *not* do something.
They can only do something.

Mother Teresa seemed to have a handle on this concept. As she said, "I will never attend an anti-war rally. If you have a peace rally, invite me."

When in doubt, stick to your brain's core competency. Rewrite the script so your emphasis becomes doing something desirable rather than avoiding the undesirable. That means every time someone implores, "Don't forget," you have my permission to haughtily reply, "I believe you meant 'remember,'" and then purposefully flounce away.

WORDS

Words are super important. I'm a writer, so take that with a grain of salt. But make it one of those hipster coarse pink Himalayan sea salts.

Do you recall words of encouragement that inspired you years ago? A circumstance when you needed a boost, and a comment or phrase stuck with you? If so, you already know the power of words. I'll bet you've done the same for others, including times you don't even remember.

Being cognizant of your words is a step in the right direction. Next is harnessing that awareness. A fine place to start is being on alert for opportunities to shift another's mind-set via well-placed, sincere, thoughtful words.

If you want your words to reach and inspire others, you may want to practice translating from Snowflake lingo to Cactus dialect and back again.

TOOLSHED MOMENT
Customizing Language

As established, Snowflakes lead from their hearts and Cacti lead from their heads. While everybody thinks and everybody feels, a dominant characteristic of Snowflakes is feeling, and a primary trait of Cacti is thinking.

As fate would have it, in many languages the foundational words "think" and "feel" are interchangeable.

Plus, it turns out Snowflakes happen to say "feel" regularly, while Cacti favor the word "think." This holds true for riffs such as "felt, feels, feelings" and "thought, thinks, thoughts."

Observations over time can reveal quite a bit about the speaker. Those who highly identify as Cacti even more strongly favor versions of the word "think," whereas strongly identified Snowflakes more readily default to variations of "feel." Some people use nearly equal amounts of thinking and feeling words. This could indicate a preference right near the middle of the spectrum.

For most, this is all on an unconscious level. But not us! You can learn to consciously vary your language choices and tap this skill to emulate others' language usage, strengthen teams, and promote ideas. Let's take a leisurely stroll down the three-phase pathway.

Phase One

Take note of when others say "think" or "feel." You need never be mind-numbingly bored in a meeting again! Now at a minimum you can enjoy yourself by keeping tallies of others' favored use of these words. In fact, you can engage in this little experiment virtually anywhere—even when you're alone (think songs, shows, movies, news commentaries, articles . . .).

DIALOGUE SAMPLE

Imagine we are eavesdropping on two recent readers of this book. Keep an eye out for words central to the core of each. Italics are our little helpers.

"C" dwells in the sand dunes of Arizona's Sonoran Desert.

"S" resides on the edge of the Arctic Circle, if you catch my drift.

Here goes nothing:

C: What are your *thoughts* on that book?

S: I *felt* like it was enlightening.

C: Do you *think* you'll be more effective now?

S: I dunno. I did appreciate the emphasis on *sensitivity*.

C: You seem plenty sensitive. I'm talking about *practical* impact.

S: Why are you shouting? You seem mad.

As you may gather, these two are speaking different languages. You might also surmise that tone also contributes to the dialogue disconnects.

Phase Two

Practice branching out to garner further insight into the brain's inner workings. This is accomplished by widening the scope of words you sort for, including the heavy hitters "sensitivity" and "practical" (as just demoed in our sample dialogue).

Here are additional words commonly utilized by each temperament:

Favored Cactus Words

Analysis	Consistency	Fairness
Logic	Practical	Pragmatic
Principle	Rationale	Validity

Favored Snowflake Words

Caring	Compassion	Empathy
Harmony	Intensity	Kind
Sensitive	Sympathetic	Wisdom

There is also what we deem nonspecific or neutral language. These words do not favor one style over the other:

Nonspecific Words

Believe	Experience	Know
Perceive	Realize	Recognize
Seem	Sense	Understand

Phase Three

Practice customizing, or interchanging, language choices. Try a few samples on for size in this practice round:

What do you think?
→
How do you feel about that?

I think that blog is worthwhile.
→
I got a positive feeling from that blog.

What did you think about the podcast?
→
How did you feel about the podcast?

I can't abide pushovers.
→
I can't abide rude people.

Conflict is healthy.
→
Conflict is stressful.

I think the class was useful.
→
I felt good about the class.

Language Dexterity

Benefits of language dexterity include:

- Building rapport with an opposite style
- Speaking to a group with diverse preferences
- Successful workplace interactions
- Promoting sales, services, and products

What can be the impact of tossing about words willy-nilly?

I overheard (who couldn't?) a seemingly hotshot (or at least opinionated) attorney in a coffee bar bellowing into his cellphone, presumably at his assistant. Apparently she had included in her legal brief a sentence that began, "The plaintiff feels . . ." The attorney lost his marbles. "I don't give a [expletive] what he feels! What occurred? What is factual?"

I suppose our legal lesson here is that feelings don't hold up in a court of law. At your lawyer audition, go for the neutral. Remember: The plaintiff experienced, understood, realized. I'm certain this will unexpectedly come in handy for you someday.

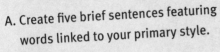

WORKSHEET: Levering Language

A. Create five brief sentences featuring words linked to your primary style.

  1.

  2.

  3.

  4.

  5.

B. Replace your typical language with neutral options.

  1.

  2.

  3.

  4.

  5.

C. Translate by replacing favored words to suit those with an opposite style.

  1.

  2.

  3.

  4.

  5.

Complimentary samples:

FOR A SNOWFLAKE

A. I felt my ideas were ignored in the meeting.

B. I believe my ideas were ignored in the meeting.

C. I think my ideas were ignored in the meeting.

FOR A CACTUS

A. It's important to analyze different viewpoints.

B. It's important to recognize different viewpoints.

C. It's important to empathize with different viewpoints.

When you wish to sway others, resist the urge to change their values. Instead, make a compelling case for what inherently resonates. Snowflakes are interested in human impact, connectivity, kindness. Cacti focus on feasibility, cost-benefit analysis, the bottom line.

When speaking to a group or those with whom you're unfamiliar, draw upon preferred lingo from both sides of the spectrum. Modifying written and verbal language to each style is a fantastic start to harness the power of linguistics.

ACTIONS

A now familiar refrain is that you cannot control other people. However, you can absolutely influence behaviors through your actions. By flexing your style (see chapter 3) you can cultivate a diverse set of behavioral options. Understanding what makes you tick is a starting, not an ending, point.

Temperament is an explanation, not an excuse.

The goal is not to proclaim, "Oh! I'm a Snowflake/Cactus! That's why I can't _____." It's the precise opposite. Strike that. Reverse it: "Oh! I'm a Snowflake/Cactus! That's why _____ is so challenging for me. My heightened awareness can translate into heightened effectiveness."

We began by addressing our thought patterns. We segue into what we say and how we say it. Which brings us here today, face to face with our actions. Specifically, exploring the benefits of making conscious behavioral choices.

Snowflakes are diplomatic, whereas Cacti are direct—this distinction embodies a defining characteristic of each camp. Yet those on each side can embody their opposite to achieve their foundational goals.

THE RUBBER HITS THE ROAD
Diplomacy or Directness?

Matthew is an English professor with a predilection for Snowflakery. He is all about diplomacy and creating a supportive classroom environment. This is challenged at times by the occasional difficult student. He describes his characteristic response as follows: "My usual strategy for behavior management is to gently get us back on track. I may make a lighthearted reference to our code of conduct, and they generally get the hint. However, last semester I had a student who continually interrupted others by jumping in with his own comments. Unless reined in, he derailed our classroom discussions. I sensed his disruptions were not intentional, yet my usual strategies didn't do the trick."

The professor's goal of fostering a collaborative atmosphere for his seminar was undermined by one student's behavior. Matthew realized that in this case his students would collectively benefit if he took a stance more typically associated with a Cactus.

"I had to adjust my style and be more direct. I took the disruptive student aside to explain they needed to listen more and give others a chance to talk. We came up with a couple strategies, and it worked."

Influencing others needn't be punitive or pushy. Better to identify and address what matters to others. This is decidedly more effective than convincing others to align with your point of view.

Personally Relevant Benefits

Is there a person whose behavior you would like to influence? Forget about demanding unrealistic modifications or offering up thinly veiled threats. Merely discern what others value and focus on their interests. *Personally relevant benefits* (PRB) vary from person to person, so this is yet another excellent opportunity to apply our Big Two model (see chapter 2).

There's a strong temptation to think we know what matters to others. We then jump headfirst into a litany of generic benefits that may or may not resonate.

For example, let's say I'm trying to convince you to taste sour cream, to which you have an aversion. I might begin by listing all the nutritional benefits, then wax eloquent about how tasty it is, making no headway. Instead, I can discern what is personally relevant to you by asking the reason why you don't want to plop a spoonful of sour cream into your exquisitely fragrant bowl of black bean soup. You immediately reply it reminds you of yogurt, which you tried once as a child and disliked. This propels me into a whole new action plan. My direction now is to explain the differences between the two, and before we know it, you're stirring a dollop into your soup.

THE RUBBER HITS THE ROAD

Meandering in Late

I was teaching an online seminar that accrued professional development course credits for the participants. The program required a nomination process to attend.

One student, Josey, consistently arrived fifteen to thirty minutes late. Because of the student-featured, interactive format, this behavior was disruptive and dismissive to her classmates. I considered making a one-on-one appointment to tell Josey she was being rude and should perhaps consider withdrawing. In the nick of time, I remembered the concept of PRB and refrained from this tactic. Instead, I began noticing clues about what was important to her. I heard her speak frequently of her myriad responsibilities and time demands. I also noticed that when in class she appeared fully engaged.

I also paid more attention to my own responses. I realized I had established a pattern of starting class a few minutes late to minimize her interruptions.

I did arrange a brief meeting with Josey. I said I noticed she was entering progressively later each day and wondered why. She explained she had to make the most of every moment of her day. Since class usually began late, she cranked out a few items from her to-do list first thing in the morning rather than showing up on time and waiting for others to arrive. I began noticing a Catch-22. I also realized her PRB was to be as efficient as possible.

I needed to make being on time match with her values. I told her I would go back to starting right on time, which synced with my own style anyway. I said I understood sometimes people had to arrive late and, while not being punitive, I also wouldn't pause the class to recap or accommodate the tardy arrival. If she continued being late, I could take responsibility through my own actions to minimize the impact on others.

She began showing up right when class started. Her behavior changed because a timely arrival now correlated with her goal of having a highly productive day.

After sharing similar scenarios, I've been asked, "What if two people who work together don't click?"

First, I'll note that is a Snowflake question. This type of concern is not on a Cactus's radar. Next, I must point out:

**Successful interactions do not depend
upon clicking with others.**

I understand this is good and bad news. On the one hand, there is no prerequisite to click with every soul who crosses your path. On the other hand, you must proceed forward on committees, teams, workgroups, and the like with people you don't "get."

I can advise people to separate emotionally; to not let people get under their skin. Cacti might reply, "Yeah, that makes sense. Good point." Not so simple for Snowflakes, for whom disassociating is the equivalent of a high-wire act. What's helpful for both sides? Accept differences and direct your collective attention to developing concrete systems for successful collaboration.

HAZARD ALERT: OVERSOFTENING THE BLOW!

An intensive version of feedback often integrated into executive coaching is called a 360. Confidential data is collected from those who interact with the coachee in a range of capacities: supervisors, coworkers, clients, and direct reports. The term 360 is short for 360 degrees, because feedback is collected in a virtual circle around the recipient.

The responses are consolidated, analyzed, and compared with the coachee's self-assessment. A challenge for the coach is to provide the data in a way that enables the recipient to learn and grow.

My colleague, Vince, told me about a time when he was delivering absolutely abysmal 360 results. The worst he'd ever seen. Figuring the recipient would be crushed, he prepared intensively.

Upon concluding the session, he glanced at his client, a volatile Cactus COO, for signs of her reaction. She burst into a wide grin, saying (direct quote), "That wasn't nearly as bad as I expected! I did great!"

Vince instantly knew that he blew it. He made the assumption his client would respond like himself, a Snowflake. He'd projected his own devastated reaction. He would have been far more successful flexing his soften-the-blow style to match the client's rough-and-tumble personality.

Several days later, Vince was slated to provide 360 feedback to another Cactus in the context of an intensive multiweek leadership development program. He delivered the results with a tough, direct approach. His client absolutely loved it, saying it was the best part of the entire program.

Different strokes for different folks.

Just as some like grit and others seek sentiment, certain people are motivated by external insights and others by inner guidance.

Enter the mantra.

TOOLSHED MOMENT
Creating a Mantra

Mantra is a Sanskrit word meaning a sacred message or text, charm, spell, or counsel. The concept of a mantra emerged from Hinduism and Buddhism as a mesmerizing sound intended to aid concentration in meditation. Through the centuries, the notion has broadened and been interpreted in numerous ways:

- Frequently repeated inspirational concept

- Motivational phrase

- Soothing rhythmic utterance

- Personal value statement

- Inner saying to shift behavior

- Slogan or motto

The mantra is a versatile tool that merges this chapter's three featured themes: thoughts, words, and actions. Why not create a mantra of your own? No pressure, as mantras are malleable and can be altered upon your whim.

Start with an intention. What aspect of your mind-set would you like to refine? Perhaps you want to rescript negative self-talk, replace beliefs that no longer serve you, or revise your daily patterns.

Consider reversing or reframing what frequently shows up in your mind. Do you have ingrained thoughts or habits you'd like to replace with healthier options?

Mantra creation begins with allowing your thoughts to flow without judgment. Find a comfortable place to write freely. Begin with a stream of consciousness, scribing whatever emerges in your mind. Do not attempt to rein in your flow of ideas. This is for an audience of one. No need to backtrack or edit what you've written.

After five to fifteen minutes of nonjudgmental writing, read through what you've written. Do patterns emerge? Does something jump out at you? Select a word or phrase that captures your attention. Consider what actions could accompany a practice mantra.

The creation and use of mantras vary thematically between Snowflakes and Cacti. For instance:

	SNOWFLAKE	CACTUS
PURPOSE	To inspire	To motivate
VALUE	Create meaning	Create structure
FOCUS	Infuse kindness	Infuse purpose

Setting up a mantra is like arranging furniture in a room. Play around with possibilities, notice the impact, and make changes as needed.

CHEAT SHEET

- *Thoughts*: Improve self-talk with the Recognize, Accept, Revise (RAR) Model.

- *Words*: Leverage the power of words through language dexterity and calibrating your use of Snowflake/Cactus dialects.

- *Actions*: Address personally relevant benefits to target what others value, forging stronger alliances.

CHAPTER SIX

Stress and Shadows

PERSONALITY IN TIMES OF ANGST

Everything that irritates us about others can lead us to an understanding of ourselves.

—CARL JUNG

POP QUIZ!
AGAIN WITH THE GENERALIZATIONS

True or False?

A Snowflake is intrinsically benevolent, gentle, and kindhearted.

A Cactus is the epitome of calm, cool, and collected.

Answers:

False again.

False.

Snowflakes feel deeply. That doesn't necessarily translate into universally positive interactions.

Cacti are guided by practicalities. That doesn't guarantee they've got it all under control.

Snowflakes can be kind and composed. They can also be volatile or high-strung. They are emotional, encompassing all kinds of feelings and reactions. They can morph into snowdrifts, ice storms, hail pellets, blizzards, and flurries. They often run in the same circles as sleet and slush.

Cacti can be rational and principled. Oft a voice of reason, when triggered they can become the proverbial bull in a china shop.

In either camp, an unsteady mindset leads to heightened agitation.

Snowflakes and Cacti alike can present at their best when in a healthy state. Even when facing difficulties, a positive state of mind can override negative reactions. Yet either personality style can become low functioning.

SHORT CIRCUITING

Everybody short-circuits at times. The outer manifestations can be similar across the board. Low-functioning Snowflakes and Cacti alike are prone to:

- Volatility
- Incessant blame
- Inability to achieve
- Negativity
- Withdrawal
- Loss of emotional control

In a nutshell, we colloquially fall to pieces. Whether we show up as our best or worst depends on multiple factors. Inner and outer dynamics interplay to make us high or low performing.

When we're doing well, our self-esteem aligns with positive connotations. Whom shall we highlight as an example? How about . . . you! Yes, the person holding this book.

I'm going to give you a psychic reading! Envision me waving my arms mysteriously over your head. May I hazard a guess about your personality?

I'm picking up on a vibe that you are a thoughtful, intelligent person. You are well intentioned and strive to be a positive influence. You're unique, creative, and poised to make a special contribution to the world.

How did I gather such razor-sharp imagery across space and time? Actually, I heard a podcast explaining what attributes resonate with almost anyone seeking a $5 palm reading and adapted the lesson for our purposes.

The descriptors I chose for our psychic encounter support a healthy self-image. It is affirming when others pick up on traits that align with our own self-perceptions. We tend to agree with them. In a peak state, your thoughts and behaviors align with a positive self-esteem.

Yet even the most well adjusted among us can slip into unfamiliar terrain, landing in a veritable abyss. At times anyone can stumble into a *grip* state.

IN THE GRIP

What does it mean to be *in the grip*? We behave out of type, contradicting our typical mannerisms. We experience unusual, out-of-character thoughts, feelings, and behaviors. Choices and resulting actions go topsy-turvy.

You may recall difficult times when you experienced an unintentional shift in your personality. Collaborative by nature, you lashed out at those around you. Pragmatic? You made illogical decisions. Typically a big-picture person, you became entrenched in details. These are a few potential indicators of falling into the grip.

As an atypical version of ourselves emerges, our behavior becomes irrational or unstable. Based on a component of Carl Jung's typology, this is called an *inferior function* experience.* Amplified by fatigue and trauma, a usually hidden aspect of our personality emerges.

THE RUBBER HITS THE ROAD
Inferior Function Takeover

A highly regarded Cactus, Micah, was invited to head up a new research facility. For this lifelong scientist, it was a dream come true. Micah's first order of business was identifying a top-notch deputy director. This was the most critical initial hiring decision to get the center off the ground. Everyone in the C-suite figured bringing Henry, the top candidate, on board was a slam dunk. He was a subject matter expert with credentials to spare.

It's hard to pinpoint precisely when things skidded off the tracks. During the closing interview, Henry rubbed Micah the wrong way. Even Micah couldn't articulate the turning point. As a career scientist, Micah had always prided himself on being uniformly pragmatic. Yet in this exceptionally demanding transition he was sleep-deprived, overwhelmed, and in the throes of a transcontinental relocation.

---

* Jung, Carl. *Memories, Dreams, Reflections.* Pantheon Books, 1973.

In a last-minute, knee-jerk decision, Micah selected a lightweight with no relevant experience to be his deputy. Two years later the executive team was still picking up the pieces from this poor hiring decision.

What causes a grip episode? Being in the grip is most likely to occur when you are under extreme pressure or an external trigger activates a severely negative internal reaction.

Stressors vary tremendously from one person to another. Identical scenarios can be experienced as pressure-inducing or motivational. Consider a time when you've seen this occur.

The same vague work assignment could undo me while propelling you into action. Giving a presentation energizes me yet conjures stress for many others. We are each tossed into the abyss for different reasons and circumstances.

Triggers

A variety of triggers can propel us into the grip of inferior function responses, including significant periods of:

- High stress
- Extreme fatigue
- Physical/psychological illness
- Major life transitions
- Feeling out of control
- Anxiety-provoking external demands
- Sudden, unanticipated, undesired change

Let's take a moment to garner additional insight from the last bullet item.

Change and Snowflakes

Most people realize sudden, unanticipated, undesirable change can provoke stress. Albeit plenty of discomfort can arise from *desired* change as well. While what is experienced as positive varies from person to person, typical desired changes can include:

- A new job or promotion

- Moving to a new home

- Starting a family

Any change is difficult because every transition inherently includes a shift in the status quo. All change includes loss, starting with the loss of the familiar. Here's the rub. So-called positive change dredges up discomfort *and* guilt for feeling bad about something "good." Snowflakes are particularly apt to suffer given their propensity for guilt. The ensuing pain can be mitigated by acknowledging these reactions and sharing them with others. Unfortunately, being in the grip is often accompanied by closing in on oneself, locking out others' support.

Additional Grip Alerts

One gauge of being in the grip is experiencing a loss of perspective. This can play out as tunnel vision, exaggerated focus, anger, or heightened emotion. In extreme circumstances we may describe the experience as "seeing red," or "It felt like my head was imploding!"

Another common sign of being in the grip is reiterating a disputed point of view in a progressively louder and more adamant tone. Under normal functioning, we recognize the limitations of such a strategy. Do I imagine shouting at you will make you spontaneously agree with my point of view? When under extreme stress, however, this behavior provides a momentary illusion of control.

The Shadows

The *shadow* facet of personality is the hidden part of ourselves with which we do not consciously identify. The term *shadow self* is used to describe when we exhibit an atypical aspect of our personality.

In times of instability we may dwell in the shadows, or unknown, part of our unconscious. This can play out in diametrically opposed ways, either contradicting or exaggerating our dominant function.

One indicator of being in a shadow state is when you embody your own opposite. The emergence of the inferior function occurs when you behaviorally contradict your dominant personality style, losing touch with your true, core self. Samples include:

- A Snowflake of epic proportions transforms into a Prickles Galore.

- A Snowflake becomes sharply critical, with no consideration for hurt feelings.

- A staunch Cactus becomes wishy-washy and irresolute.

- A Cactus becomes driven by emotion, with no rational foundation.

The second manifestation is indicated by overuse of one's primary function, an amplified display of one's usual characteristics. We become off-the-rail versions of ourselves.

Exaggeration of one's leading style could be exhibited as:

- A Snowflake incessantly asking for positive reinforcement

- A Snowflake obsessively concerned with moods, ceaselessly inquiring how others are feeling

- A Cactus continually provoking others, picking fights at any opportunity

- A Cactus relentlessly pushing a Snowflake to toughen up, while hurling insults

Shadow Styles

Want to increase the likelihood of tumbling into the grip? How about finding yourself amid a pandemic? Recall a few pages back the list of triggers that are among the most likely to put us in danger of a downward spiral. Nearly all align with living in a pandemic, including dealing with rapid, unanticipated, unwanted change. As the 2020 pandemic unfolded, I noticed a range of responses. We'll look at four prevalent themes, including ensuing patterns.

Theme One: Practicality—Cactus
FOCUS: Problem solving

MANIFESTATION: Accept things are different and move along.

WHAT CAN INFURIATE: Sole focus on practical issues can backfire.

SUBTEXT: "Suck it up and pull yourself together."

Theme Two: Frozen with Empathy—Snowflake
FOCUS: People's feelings

MANIFESTATION: Acutely aware of lost dreams, even for people you've never met.

WHAT CAN INFURIATE: Panicking. Weeping.

SUBTEXT: "A sinking feeling."

Theme Three: Platitudes—Mix of Snowflake + Cactus

FOCUS: Superficial, inept platitudes. Sugarcoating.

MANIFESTATION: Start a gratitude journal! An ending is a new beginning!

WHAT CAN INFURIATE: Dismisses emotional responses and invalidates personal suffering.

SUBTEXT: "You have no right to complain; others have it much worse."

Fortunately, a fourth theme also emerged; however, it was less prevalent.

Theme Four: Affirmation— Evolved Mix of Snowflakes + Cacti

FOCUS: Validation of subjective experiences without comparisons.

MANIFESTATION: Realism; recognition of individual loss without judgment.

WHY IT DOESN'T INFURIATE: Whereas the other three drive a wedge between the speaker and listener, this version brings people relief and mutual support.

SUBTEXT: "Be kind to yourself."

The first three behavioral themes feature suppression, immobility, and denial. The final theme faces reality while honoring the real challenges being faced.

Breaking Free

If you're already in the grip, practicing going into a meta-state can alleviate the symptoms somewhat. (See "Reframing Reactions" in chapter 4.)

Prepare for the near inevitability of an occasional grip experience by cultivating awareness of what builds you up and what breaks you down. This will help reduce the intensity of any future episodes.

WORKSHEET: Self-Analysis

Find a quiet place to sit with minimal distractions. Take a few deep breaths and bring your focus inward. What you scribe may not sync with standard adages or typical advice from others. Consider what rings true in your core. You are your best guide.

What energizes you?

_____

_____

_____

What stresses you?

_____

_____

_____

What qualities describe you at your best? What are you like when you are most yourself?

_____

_____

_____

WORKSHEET: Self-Analysis *continued*

When you're not yourself, how are you different from usual? What provokes these changes?

_____

_____

_____

What activities, people, or places help you reestablish normalcy?

_____

_____

_____

Completing the Self-Analysis Worksheet is a gift to your future self. Thoughtful processing of what makes you tick will help pave the way back to clarity when most needed.

The Upside

When all is said and done, we can extract value from descending into, and returning from, the grip. Benefits can include

- A signal to make positive change
- A warning of doing too much
- An opportunity for growth and development
- An ability to better understand the unconscious
- Enhanced self-awareness
- Greater control of thoughts and feelings

OTHERS IN SHADOW

As you may surmise, you're not the sole human suscepti-
ble to sliding into the occasional grip experience. Most of us
are. That means there's an exceedingly high chance you'll
encounter others from time to time who seem out of whack.
That may or may not be a medical term.

What Are the Signs?

First: Look for signs that another person could be off-kilter.
Perhaps a person you regularly engage with is acting in strange
or unexpected ways. If someone is behaving out of character,
they could be in the grip of an inferior function experience.

Then: Calibrate your observations against their usual behavior. If a soccer coach is consistently unnerved in the final
moments of the game, this is simply his modus operandi. If
a sublimely serene tennis instructor starts berating students
for losing a match, that merits taking notice.

THE RUBBER HITS THE ROAD
Skid Marks

Shirley owned a small storefront kitchen
goods shop featuring a compact demonstration kitchenette.
Providing freshly made food samples and hosting cooking
demonstrations was her favorite part of the business. When
COVID-19 struck, she was forced to close up the cooking
area. Each time she walked into the store she got a sinking
feeling in her stomach.

Her gregarious personality turned in on itself. She began
snapping at vendors and spending most of her time in
the back storage area rather than greeting customers.

Exhausted, she convinced herself to stop caring about the shop altogether.

Her lifelong friend Donna came by to visit. Others, with superficial ties, could explain away Shirley's despondency as lack of resilience. Donna knew better. She recognized Shirley was exhibiting entirely atypical behavior. Yet Donna sensed her good intentions were backfiring. Nothing seemed to help.

What to do? Someone you know is flying off the proverbial handle. You want to help defuse the situation. Easier said than done. Many natural responses backfire. Let's explore six common attempts to "cheer someone up" and how they play out.

Then I'll offer up some useful alternatives.

Backfire Central

Abysmal Technique #1
It's not so bad.
INTENTION
Convince them everything is basically fine. Downplay the situation.
ENACTMENT
"It's not worth worrying. Everyone survives a computer crash."

Abysmal Technique #2
Pull it together.
INTENTION
Restore normalcy, calm them down.
ENACTMENT
"Cool it, take a chill pill."

Abysmal Technique #3
Commiserate.

INTENTION
Demonstrate over-the-top sympathy.

ENACTMENT
"That is horrible! I can't believe that happened to you. How can you stand it?"

Abysmal Technique #4
Overidentify.

INTENTION
Prove that you can relate.

ENACTMENT
"I know exactly how you feel. Let me tell you about this time when I got super frustrated."

Abysmal Technique #5
Teasing or sarcasm.

INTENTION
Make light of the situation.

ENACTMENT
"Yeah, I bet this is the first fridge ever to spring a leak on a holiday weekend."

Abysmal Technique #6
Attempt to reason.

INTENTION
Convince them to be rational.

ENACTMENT
"All businesses have rough patches. Focus on solutions."

A Variation on Abysmal Technique #2

This one can rear its head in a wide range of backdrops, such as:

A first-year medical student failed her first exam of the year. Distraught, she made her way to office hours of the physician who taught the course. She shuffled in, head down. No sooner did she mention her failing grade than an unwelcome tear skidded down her cheek. The professor, trained by his own Cactus research advisor, told her to not be so upset. "Toughen up!" he recommended.

She silently determined she wouldn't attend his office hours again.

Additional Words on Abysmal Technique #5

Making light, joking around, or playful teasing are go-to behaviors for many. This approach usually backfires. Only indulge if you know the person exceedingly well. I've seen defaulting to sarcasm ruin relationships and endanger careers.

Why They're All Abysmal

All six of these popular techniques fall short, despite earnest intentions of the implementers. Each backfires for a combination of the following:

- Invalidates others' experiences
- Minimizes and dismisses concerns
- Contradicts their thoughts and feelings
- Makes them feel even worse
- Redirects attention to you
- Triggers a counterreaction
- Creates a divide between the two of you

Here's the double whammy:

The person in question is upset *and* being told they're wrong for being upset.

Resultingly, the already agitated person can feel alienated, misunderstood, and inadequate. Do not despair; there is hope. Preparation opens options to right the boat.

A Useful Set of Responsive Options

Acquaint yourself with these sublime alternative responses. They needn't be delivered in the order listed.

1. Ask How You Can Be Helpful

Recollect the medical student scenario. If you find yourself in the teaching physician's shoes, here's a quick recommendation. Replace "Toughen up!" with "How can I be helpful to you?" Then sit back and allow the student time to process and reply. Resist making your own suggestions. I'll bet she asks for a lot less than you may have offered. This elegant technique is worth its weight in gold and a real time-saver.

2. Validate Concerns

Honor others' desire to be understood. Expressing an understanding of another's perspective is not the same as agreeing with or promoting their point of view. A supportive "I can see you're upset" is a fine start.

3. Maintain Emotional Separation

Prevent your own feelings from being sucked into the vortex. Are you listening, Snowflakes? You will be most helpful by keeping your emotions in check. While working in consumer advocacy, I could resolve twice as many cases by implementing this approach.

4. Establish Intellectual Distance

Rather than debating the worthiness of practical solutions, be a supportive sounding board for others' thoughts and ideas. This is neither the time nor the place for intellectual discourse. And I say that as retired captain of the high school debate team.

5. Encourage Them to Develop Strategies

This is the most likely path to ensure the strategies take hold. It also means you don't have to come up with all the bright ideas. At the same time, offer tangible support when possible.

6. Follow Up on Promises

Underpromise and overdeliver. Pause before overcommitting. If you make an offer, follow through. Good intentions without fulfillment can morph into a loss of credibility. Afraid you'll drop the ball? Set a reminder or ask for one.

A FINE POINT

Behaving as your own opposite isn't inherently problematic. What matters is whether this conduct is subconscious and destructive or conscious and intentional. When deliberate and purposeful, behaving "out of type" can enable you to obtain your goals.

Crisis hotlines require volunteers steadfastly commit to disentangling from others' crises. They are populated nearly entirely by Snowflakes, looking to achieve a higher purpose. These otherwise prototypical Snowflakes are trained to remain stalwart. By embodying some of the best Cactus traits, the Snowflake volunteers become successful counselors.

- *For yourself:* It's normal to slip into the grip at times. Be kind to yourself.

- *For others:* Squelch the urge to blurt out, "Calm down!" Focus on others' point of view.

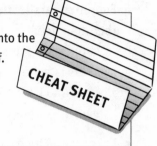

CHAPTER SEVEN

Leaders in the Tundra and Sahara

METHODS TO MAXIMIZE LEADERSHIP EFFECTIVENESS

Inspiration is for amateurs—the rest of us just show up and get to work.

—CHUCK CLOSE

POP QUIZ!
SWITCH-A-ROO?

Question: Does Tough Snowflake = Cactus?

Answer: Nope.

Snowflakes proficient at leveraging a range of behaviors are flexible Snowflakes; they do not spontaneously transform into Cacti. And vice versa.

Cacti and Flakers alike abound in the leadership arena. No credible data suggests either is inherently a more successful leader. Everyone has their own peculiar propensities.

Leadership Characteristics

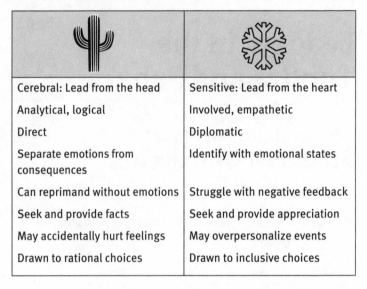

Cerebral: Lead from the head	Sensitive: Lead from the heart
Analytical, logical	Involved, empathetic
Direct	Diplomatic
Separate emotions from consequences	Identify with emotional states
Can reprimand without emotions	Struggle with negative feedback
Seek and provide facts	Seek and provide appreciation
May accidentally hurt feelings	May overpersonalize events
Drawn to rational choices	Drawn to inclusive choices

Did you find your spot among the array of leadership characteristics? Kudos! You're an exemplary, self-aware leader.

You don't get the rest of the day off. Quite the contrary. Now you get to be on high alert for the subtle clues of employees, supervisors, teammates, and clients regarding how they engage in the world. Let's get busy!

Being adaptive is a particularly clutch quality for those in leadership positions. There's a high likelihood you've got a haphazard arrangement of prickly spikes and crystalized snow among your team. If you are a Cactus amid a crew of Snowflakes, learning to speak their language will take you far. Reverse that for Snowflake leaders.

You'll also be seeking different motivators for each. Did you say, "Summary please?" I'm on it!

Snowflake—What Resonates and Motivates

Recognition	Benevolence	Encouragement

Cactus—What Resonates and Motivates

Fairness	Justice	Intelligence

You may discover a member (or two) of your team has the exact opposite composition as you. That's wonderful news. This person can be a tremendous asset. For example, if you're a Snowflake, after staff meetings you can confer with your Cactus ally for analytical insights you may have missed. A Cactus can check in with a Snowflake collaborator regarding the state of participants' underlying emotions.

Are You for Real?

A quick vignette. A Cactus named Nadia joined in on a conference call with Claude, a Snowflake. Upon her entry, he was gushing about a coworker's presentation. In Nadia's mind, the presentation had been mediocre. It was ridiculous for Claude to be so over the top. For Nadia to gush like that would have indubitably been manufactured. She assumed this applied to anyone and that Claude was only trying to impress their supervisor with his gung-ho style. Frankly, it annoyed her. The next day she told him.

Let's start with the elephant in the room. If a Snowflake sincerely feels continual, effusive gratitude, can there be a downside to expressing it?

Praise Galore

Snowflakes are all about positive reinforcement. It flows forth naturally. Makes sense, as they themselves are highly motivated by praise. Yet, sadly, this can backfire. Free flowing compliments have a diminishing collective impact. Cacti roll their eyes thinking, *Sure, that's Devora; she gushes over everyone.* (You have no reason to deduce I'm referring to myself. A serendipitous namesake.)

Even worse, folks with cerebral natures may find it impossible that such abundant praise could be sincere. That's right . . . now you're under suspicion of being a phony. A devastating label to bestow on an earnest Snowflake.

Meanwhile, think back to a time when you were the rare recipient of positive feedback from a formidable Cactus. Even a perfunctory comment may stick in your mind indefinitely when it is offered up like a rare gem.

The upshot is that curmudgeonly Cacti get more bang for their buck due to product scarcity (the product being the praise). Meanwhile, the Snowflake's accolades get brushed aside, while the softy Snowflake is called into question for continual compliments.

Cruel fate!

THE RUBBER HITS THE ROAD

"You're #1!"

Isaac is a project lead in a manufacturing plant. The place is teeming with Cacti. Efficiency is king, with top industry awards proudly lining in the hallways.

Isaac seems to be the lone Snowflake this side of Human Resources. Getting to headquarters from his building requires a shuttlebus ride across the main campus. He views this ten-minute ride as an extra opportunity to dispense praise to others on the bus.

Isaac believes in the power of kudos down to his core. Last year's holiday gifts to his team were water bottles embossed with "You Are a Star!" His coffee mug, refilled several times a day, proclaims "Catch them doing it right!" in neon bubble lettering.

Isaac holds weekly team meetings and hosts quarterly departmental townhalls. He is an easy target at the annual holiday party roasts. Isaac renditions are fan favorites: "Hey there . . . seeing you makes my day!" "You're such a special person!" "Your hard work means so much to me." Isaac wholeheartedly joins in on the laughter.

TOOLSHED MOMENT
Earnest Effusions

How can a Snowflake's effusions have the desired effect? Nobody wants to have their earnest acclamations categorically dismissed. Least of all a Snowflake.

Behold! Tips for the taking. Let's kick it off with . . .

A. Know your crowd:
Attune your degree of enthusiasm to the recipients. A flurry of Snowflakes has a decidedly higher tolerance for effusiveness than a grove of Cacti. Tolerate is not quite the word. It's more on the nose to say Snowflakes *crave* it.

B. Know your crowd deux:
Give praise that resonates. When telling a Cactus the impact of bringing bagels to the office to kick off a demanding week, replace "You made everyone happy!" with "That really motivated people to double down on their efforts."

C. If you don't know your crowd:
Snowflakes: Err toward assuming Cacti are abundant. Dial it back a smidge.
Cacti: Toss in a few words of appreciation. Amp it up a notch.

D. Be specific:
Resist clichés ("You're the best!"). Replace with personalized observations ("You have a rare talent for defusing tension in stressful meetings").

E. Pay attention to time and place:
At a quarterly review, timely feedback goes a lot further than sweeping generalizations. Also, consider when praise is best delivered one-on-one rather than in front of others.

F. Less is more:
While it pains me to say so, overdone praise has diminishing marginal returns.

Know Yourself

When people radiate positive reinforcement, this nearly always correlates with craving it themselves. If you identified with Isaac, it can't hurt to do a little self-examination around your own need for praise. An insatiable appetite for glowing feedback is likely unrealistic.

If you have a "never enough" appetite for accolades, consider techniques to internally generate positive reinforcement. Heightening your level of self-acceptance also helps. Ideas can be adopted from from "Self-Talk" (see chapter 5.)

FEEL-GOOD, DO-GOOD

While there are endless methods to motivate others, the feel-good, do-good model is one of my favorites—and staunchly reflective of Snowflake and Cactus partialities. The feel-good camp, led by the pom-pom adorned Snowflakes, focuses on how people feel. The do-good faction, led by Cacti carrying clipboards, focuses on results.

HAZARD ALERT: ATTENTION SNOWFLAKE LEADERSHIP!

A feel-good leader is intent upon ensuring others feel good—about themselves, their accomplishments, their team, and, yes, their leadership. Snowflakes descend on this style like birds to scattered seeds. Who can blame them? After all, they have deeply rooted inclinations to fuel positive emotional states. Feel-good leaders emphasize a safe, supportive environment conducive to open sharing of emotions and opinions.

Except . . . brace yourself. Taken too far, the feel-good methodology can backfire. When mediocre outcomes are lauded, the impetus to excel gets squashed. If a proverbial pat on the back is doled out for lackluster effort, I am befuddled. My job becomes unstimulating, my supervisor seems disengaged, and I feel ho-hum. Extreme feel-good leadership demoralizes those it intends to motivate.

Best of Both

As a Snowflake, you'll gravitate toward encouragement. As a Cactus, you'll gravitate toward systems. Integrating components of each methodology can generate particularly strong, motivated teams.

I've seen feel-good leaders push their teams beyond original expectations. I've also observed do-good leaders cheering on their team for smashing through goals. There is cross-pollination. Each style can be infused with and enriched by best practices from the other camp.

HAZARD ALERT: ATTENTION CACTUS LEADERSHIP!

Given a propensity for tough love, minus the love part, certain leadership techniques are a natural draw for Cacti. Among them, you guessed it, is do-good leadership. Cacti are not enticed by anything in the vicinity of coddling. The do-good style really can propel folks to *do* better. Rather than offering up a bland "Go for it," the do-good leader targets a challenging yet achievable goal and coaches the team to excel through carefully calibrated encouragement.

In a crazy twist, do-good leadership can even make us feel better about ourselves than the feel-good tactics.

Although, taken to an extreme, do-good leadership can backfire. Simply instructing others to hit the mark misses the mark! People are motivated by *supported* challenges. Do you demonstrate credibility? Is there reason to believe they can meet your lofty goals? Do you have their back?

OPPORTUNITIES FOR IMPROVEMENT

The dreaded "opportunity for improvement" part of performance reviews. That's colloquial for "You're about to get some constructive criticism." Or shall we narrow it down to corrective feedback? Or, if we're short on time, criticism?

Critical feedback—Oh boy! Let's get down to it! Cacti are on board. Snowflakes scoot outside, preparing to assemble a protective structure, like an igloo.

WORKSHEET: Memorable Coach

Take a moment to recall a person who made a positive, lasting imprint on your life. Perhaps this person was a coach, educator, family member, mentor, counselor, or boss. The commonality is that this person was, for a period of time, the quintessential wind beneath your wings. Unless you're a penguin. Or, perchance, an ostrich.

While this person could have served in a range of actual roles, we'll whittle it down to *coach*.

Name or moniker of my coach: _____

Reasons—large or small—this person leapt to mind:
1.
2.

Ways they inspired or motivated me to excel:
1.
2.

Memorable moments, notable characteristics, or quirky style:
1.
2.

How my coach exhibited feel-good and do-good characteristics:
_____

_____

Ways I can support, encourage, and inspire others:
_____

_____

Even positive feedback does not attract universal adoration. "Affirmative reinforcement" is in danger of making the highly affiliated Cactus uncomfortable, skeptical, irritated, and even queasy.

Impactful feedback is not one-size-fits-all. You want the feedback recipient to be capable of processing and responding to your input. That means customized delivery is a priority. I present to you four scenarios for your consideration.

SAMPLE DIALOGUES: BELLY FLOPS AND SWAN DIVES

 SNOWFLAKE ADMINISTERING ANNUAL PERFORMANCE REVIEW TO CACTUS, MONDAY MORNING.

Take 1: Belly Flop

S: Great to see you! Been way too long!

C: Uh, hello.

S: You look great—nice orange sweater.

C: [Looks down at sweater, having forgotten which one it is. Wonders if it's against corporate policy to comment on an employee's appearance.]

C: Thanks. [Wonders when things will get started. Begins tapping pen on armrest.]

S: Anyways, I always look forward to these reviews. If nothing else, an opportunity for quality time.

SILENCE.

S: So! Let's get started. I'll begin by saying what an asset you are for our team. You're super helpful and a hard worker. I want you to know how much I appreciate that! So do the others on the team. If you've wondered what people say behind your back, now you know! [Laughs]

C: You were talking about me to the other teammates behind my back?

    S: Not really. I was kidding.

    C: [Exasperated] Got it.

What backfired and why? _____

_____

 SNOWFLAKE ADMINISTERING ANNUAL PERFORMANCE REVIEW TO CACTUS, MONDAY MORNING.

Take 2: Swan Dive

S: Good morning.

C: Good morning.

S: As you know, today is your annual performance review. I've spent time reviewing your work over the past year and have identified three key areas for improvement.

C: Fantastic.

What worked and why? _____

_____

 CACTUS ADMINISTERING ANNUAL PERFORMANCE REVIEW TO SNOWFLAKE, MONDAY MORNING.

Take 1: Belly Flop

C: As you know, today is your performance review.

S: [Gulps] Yes, I'm a bit nervous.

C: Why? Haven't you put forward your best effort? If so, there's nothing to worry about. Is there something I should be aware of?

S: What? No. I mean, I've worked hard.

C: That's all well and good, although today is about results. What are some areas you think you could have improved on this past year?

S: Umm, I guess, you tell me. [Breaks into a cold sweat]

What backfired and why? _____

_____

CACTUS ADMINISTERING ANNUAL PERFORMANCE REVIEW TO SNOWFLAKE, MONDAY MORNING.

Take 2: Swan Dive

C: Good morning! It's the big day, your annual review. Overall, I'm very pleased with your performance.

S: Wow, that's great. I'm glad to hear it.

C: You continue to exceed expectations. That said, there are a few key areas for development that I think we can target in the year ahead.

S: Of course, that sounds good. Let me know what you have in mind.

What worked and why? _____

_____

What doesn't work are communication disconnects. There is no single way to administer feedback. Finding a style that enables the receiver to hear and process what you have to say is vital to a successful conversation. Offering feedback doesn't necessarily go in one direction. At times you'll find yourself in a position to give feedback to peers and supervisors as well.

THE RUBBER HITS THE ROAD

Managing Up

Mark, a soulful Snowflake, is on a lifelong pursuit of self-actualization. He attends spiritual retreats where he learns a variety of methods to address interpersonal conflict. One such technique, dubbed a "clearing," provides a system to dissipate negative patterns without ascribing blame. Language structures attribute responsibility to oneself rather than blaming others, such as, "The story I tell myself is . . ." We'll save the nuts and bolts for a magazine insert.

Mark's biweekly men's support group often integrates clearings into their meetings. He sees a direct correlation between clearings and open, positive interactions.

By day, Mark is an account executive at a tech startup. His boss, Zoe, has a no-holds-barred personality that drains him. He's tired of all the psychic energy he puts into managing his inner responses to her brash nature. He knows it's not about him; she engages with her entire team the same way. He admires how others apparently let her style effortlessly roll off their backs.

Eventually, he acknowledged the need to confront her.

He arrived on time to their appointment, forced a smile, and dove in: "Zoe, the story I tell myself when you bark orders at me . . ." He lost her from moment one. She broke in, "You tell yourself stories about me? Really? And they involve barking orders?"

Lost in translation. While clearings are valuable models in certain environs, this type of conversing doesn't hold water in Zoe's world. This version of feedback did not yield Mark's desired results. He needed to recalibrate, so Zoe could understand the underlying issues.

In an alternative approach, he aligned himself with Zoe's nature. (If he was unclear on her style, he could apply the Big Two: observe and ask, conveniently nestled within chapter 2.)

Queue up for Mark's new and improved version of feedback:

"Hey, Zoe, thanks for taking the time to talk. I know you're super-invested in our team's success, and I appreciate your all-in personality. I've learned a ton from you.

"At the same time, I notice I shut down when you raise your voice, to the point where I can't process what you intend to convey. I've been thinking about alternative ways for us to communicate effectively. I definitely want to learn how to work at full capacity during stressful times. I wrote down some possibilities for us to review." To be continued.

What did Mark do well in his second version of feedback? Plenty.

Mark flexed his style, adapting to a method that Zoe could process. He implemented the Platinum Rule, meeting her where she's at. He employed a variation on the phrase "Is it possible?" People don't like to deny something is possible.

He kept it short and well planned so he didn't ramble. He came to his supervisor with potential solutions rather than a lengthy list of what wasn't working. He blamed no one. He provided Zoe with a written summary of ideas for her to look over before jumping into a discussion. High five, Mark!

Merging a combination of communication strategies works well for all sorts of situations, including managing up. Whether a Snowflake or a Cactus, adapting your behavior for the greater good comes in handy. Remember our earlier treatise that personalities are explanations for preferences, not excuses for falling short? Reminds me of when people blame having a poor memory for lack of follow-through. Most of us have faulty memories! The idea is to recognize your memory is unreliable and therefore create systems to keep track of your obligations.

THE RUBBER HITS THE ROAD
Flaker Gone Rogue

Janice worked for a town center development that was created to build a sense of community among local residents. Front and center was a plaza for events held throughout the year. Janice worked in the finance department and was not privy to the discussions and decisions of the senior leadership team.

She enjoyed the complementary live music provided Thursday, Friday, and Saturday evenings. She also appreciated that this feature attracted bigger crowds, which directly correlated with increased revenue. The long-standing Thursday band was widely regarded as the weak link, falling back on cliché music with a small repertoire of dated songs. Most local residents agreed the band's quality had steadily eroded.

Eventually Janice noticed the center ceased its Thursday concerts, reducing the offering to two nights a week. On a lunch break with the CFO Ricardo, Janice casually inquired about the change. Ricardo sighed and asked if Janice had ever met Stan, the vice president of community events. Janice had not.

Ricardo explained the backstory. It turned out Stan had worked with Thursday's band for years and couldn't bring himself to inform them that they were going to be replaced with a new group. Stan's solution to avoid discomfort? He decided to eliminate *any* entertainment on Thursdays, so the band wouldn't take it personally. To avoid a perceived slight, Stan diminished a cherished amenity.

If asked, Stan would have explained he "felt too bad" being "insensitive" to the presumed feelings of the Thursday night band members. All Snowflake language. Yet being a Snowflake does not take one off the hook for handling unpleasant responsibilities. When there's a responsibility to a bigger picture, it gives Snowflakes a bad name to blame their guilt for making weak decisions. Snowflakes are not wimps, and wimps are not representative of Snowflakes.

Stan seems to have a strong affinity for the Snowflake style. This could be one reason why it was particularly difficult for him to end a long-standing contract. At the same time, this absolutely does not translate into an excuse for cutting out a third of the musical programming in the community develop-ment. Furthermore, he could have been projecting his own sen-sitivities onto the band members. Who's to say they weren't Cacti and ready to move on? And if they were Snowflakes? He still needed to address the underlying issues. A more skilled leader than Stan would have picked up on "style hints" and adapted his messaging. And would certainly not have can-celled a well-regarded benefit to the local community to avoid engaging in a potentially difficult conversation.

What if you had been in a position to help Stan better manage the challenge he faced? You could have used a com-bination of do-good and feel-good coaching, helped him take into account the big picture, and offered to practice a couple run-throughs to prepare him for the upcoming discussion.

Practice makes closer to perfect. And support for teammates goes a long way. Just remember, preferences for support vary by style.

THE RUBBER HITS THE ROAD
No Sweat!

Leon was thrilled to begin his role as director of human resources for a credit card company. His first day on the job coincided with the rollout of a reorg including a redistribution of office spaces. This was Leon's first encounter with most of the staff. Leon was tasked with directing employees to new—often inferior—workstations. Well-appointed office space was sought after and scarce. As the drama amped up, two employees were inadvertently assigned to the same office space. Leon now faced the unenviable task of assigning it to one over the other, a decision certain to upset either or both parties.

The department's senior vice president, Jonah, caught the tail end of the morning chaos. He approached Leon, saying, "That looked challenging. I'm sorry you had to deal with all of it." Leon looked up, surprised, albeit undeniably calm. He smiled at Jonah. "Oh, no problem at all. These things happen!"

A Cactus, Leon felt none of the angst that Jonah filtered in via osmosis. Leon was energized by the challenges he faced.

Jonah reminded himself of three useful points. One, his own deeply rooted reactions to perceived conflict are not universal. Two, this is ultimately a good thing, as we are each best suited for different tasks. Three, hire your opposites!

A startling surfeit of "how to boom your business" advisories profess you must assume a plethora of mysterious leadership traits to succeed. This fuels a misperception that we must shelve our true natures to be five-star leaders. This is foolhardy and inevitably flops. The reverse is true. Let's be trailblazers, bringing ourselves to the table.

No need to deny your temperament, ever.

The path to success—however you define it—is blending authenticity with receptivity.

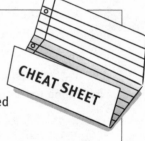

- Be an adaptive leader. Leverage natural strengths while customizing communication.

- A robust toolkit includes a blended style and skilled feedback.

CHAPTER EIGHT

Introverts and Extroverts in the Mix

THE INTERPLAY OF INTROVERSION, EXTROVERSION, SNOWFLAKES & CACTI

Be kind. For everybody you know is fighting a great battle.

—PHILO OF ALEXANDRIA

EXPANDING OUR HORIZONS

Let's shake things up. There are Snowflakes. There are Cacti. As we discovered earlier, gradations of affiliation exist for each of us. To keep things lively, many additional factors influence our dispositions. However, to prevent head explosions from overtaxed brains, this modest volume will explore just one additional nuance of personality. I promise.

Introversion and extroversion, as featured in *Networking for People Who Hate Networking* (2nd edition, Berrett Koehler, 2019), have tremendous impact on our inner and outer worlds. You are correct; the latter is at times spelled *extraversion*. This is not a typo, although I appreciate your attention to detail.*

This chapter is devoted to the interplay of Snowflakery/ Cacticury and introversion/extroversion (I/E). There are introverted Snowflakes, extroverted Snowflakes, extroverted Cacti, and introverted Cacti. Degree of preference affects the result, like the ratio of olive oil (introvert) to balsamic (extrovert) in a handcrafted salad dressing. Accented with Dijon (Cactus) and honeycomb (Snowflake).

There is not necessarily a correlation between these components. All Snowflakes are not predisposed to be introverts or extroverts, nor is a Cactus more or less likely to be an extrovert or introvert. Yet the way we each show up in the world is affected by the interplay of these four characteristics. The juxtaposition of each combination influences our underlying functioning.

101 Course

If you're not clear on the inner machinations of I/E, you are far from alone.

Innumerable false stereotypes accompany the I/E dimension. For instance: Confidence, drive, and energy level are often purported to coincide with extroversion, yet links do not exist. It's better to stroll into this chapter as a tabula rasa than as a misdirected know-it-all.

Let's devote a few moments to clearing things up. Each characteristic is delineated here, accompanied by corollaries.

---

* In Latin, "extra" means "outside" and "intro" means "inside." Carl Jung used the spelling "extravert" because extraverts turn outward, whereas introverts turn inward. Popularized in 1918, extrovert became the general predominate spelling. Now that I've made my point, we'll employ the more modern style.

INTROVERTS . . .	EXTROVERTS . . .
Energize alone	Energize with others
Corollary: Prefer one-on-one interactions	Corollary: Prefer group interactions
Think to talk	Talk to think
Corollary: Process to reach decisions	Corollary: Speak to determine decisions
Go deep (focused)	Go wide (expansive)
Corollary: Prefer selected stimuli	Corollary: Prefer numerous stimuli

These are the broad strokes; there's lots more enticing stuff to unpack. We're in the "wrapping your head around the fundamentals" portion of the program. While we're in the groove, here's another, even more concise distinction:

Extroverts collect, introverts connect.

Extroverts tend to collect experiences, people, and business cards, for instance. Introverts prefer fewer, deeper connections, interests, and activities. Introverts are disposed to stick with what they hold near and dear—from friendships to vacation spots. One introvert sagely summarized his philosophy on life thus: "Find the best, enjoy, repeat." An extrovert is more likely to seek novelty and an expanding range of experiences.

If you've arrived equipped with a background in this area, you may already know your placement on this continuum. Otherwise, if you're curious where you land on the I/E spectrum, follow this footnote for a fine place to discover your affiliation with extroverts, introverts, and centroverts.*

* *Networking for People Who Hate Networking.* 2nd ed. Berrett-Koehler, 2019.

I/E adds a robust ingredient to self-awareness, enabling you to bring the best of your sweet self to the party. For introverts, that implies a gathering of two.

Ready to rally? Let's mosey into the biosphere where introversion and extroversion mingle with our pals the Snowflake and the Cactus.

Combining Preferences

Just as a beloved combo meal draws upon the taste palate of individual flavors, the interaction of personality traits gives us each a unique flair. I find it enlightening, enjoyable, and even freeing to learn about our own inimitable personas.

As a bonus, understanding others' blends of preferences is a soothing balm for relationship flare-ups. At the time of printing, no X-ray exists to reveal inner temperaments. So how do we proceed? By picking up on clues, sprinkled like breadcrumbs in the forest, awaiting our attention. Most people trample right over them. But not us! Strap on those all-weather boots.

These clues reveal others' interests, desires, concerns, and drivers. The malady of distracted living causes many to be missed.* Paying attention pays off big-time.

Let's start simple.

ONE-WORD REPRESENTATION:

Extroverted Snowflake → Open
Introverted Snowflake → Complex
Extroverted Cactus → Opinionated
Introverted Cactus → Cloistered

---

* *Singletasking*. Berrett-Koehler, 2015.

Layers Upon Layers

As we've learned from our Snowflake and Cactus friends, diversity reigns supreme. Each of us flourishes by accepting and building from our essence.

Now, like a well-crafted shortcake, we add delectable layers to the mix. With the slight detail that they represent introverts and extroverts rather than sliced strawberries and whipped cream.

The crux of the matter is that taking stock of these additional components enriches our understanding of each other.

Overlaying two personality factors enables us to look at permutations. No time like the present. And no topics are as central to these combos as *feelings* and *opinions*.

Feelings and Opinions

	SNOWFLAKE	CACTUS
INTROVERT	*Feelings* run deep and are often kept under wraps.	*Opinions* are shared if asked for, while privately analytical.
EXTROVERT	*Feelings* cascade out. Freely and openly share emotional states.	*Opinions* flow forth with a vengeance, even if controversial.

Let's break it down further, through the lenses of behaviors and roadblocks—topped off by customized acronyms.

CHARACTERISTIC BEHAVIORS:

Extroverted Snowflake	→	Loads of communication
Introverted Snowflake	→	Ongoing self-reflection
Extroverted Cactus	→	Open sharing of shortcomings and irritations
Introverted Cactus	→	Inquisitive stream of questions when sparked

POTENTIAL ROADBLOCK:

Extroverted Snowflake	→ Difficulty keeping secrets
Introverted Snowflake	→ Internalized interactions
Extroverted Cactus	→ Sudden verbal rampages
Introverted Cactus	→ Withdrawal when rubbed the wrong way

TARGETED ACRONYMS:

Extroverted Snowflake	→ TMI (Too much information)
Introverted Snowflake	→ QTIP (Quit taking it personally)
Extroverted Cactus	→ WAIT (Why am I talking?)
Introverted Cactus	→ KISS (Keep it simple, stupid)

Clearly each combination offers unique characteristics and benefits. Each also faces particular challenges. It is easy to fall in the trap of viewing others as luckier, smarter, or happier than ourselves. Despite outer trappings, none of this is necessarily accurate. One thing we all have in common is that we each have battles to fight. Another is that many take place within, hidden from inquiring eyes.

POP QUIZ!
Disconnects

A. Who is most likely to say no immediately upon hearing a new idea?

Answer: Introverted Cactus

Why? An introverted Cactus needs time to process before agreeing to changes and therefore perceives it as safer to initially respond in the negative. Plus, introverted Cacti don't fret over offending others by saying no.

Impact on others: May acquire a reputation for being negative.

POP QUIZ!
Disconnects *continued*

B. Who it is most likely to rub the wrong way:

Answer: Extroverted Snowflake

Why? An extroverted Snowflake is apt to enthusiastically suggest new ideas and feel hurt if they are rejected.

Tip: When preparing to suggest a new concept, begin by introducing it in writing prior to meeting up. This gives everyone (particularly introverted Cacti) the opportunity to consider the proposed change in advance and ponder pros and cons. Prepare to be amazed by the shift in response from potential naysayers.

C. Who are most likely to have differing perceptions of what was agreed to in a discussion?

Answer: An extroverted Cactus and an introverted Snowflake

Why? Extroverted Cacti are predisposed to blurt out ideas without much forethought. They won't think it's necessary to filter for the potential impact on others, as they are "talking to think." Spouting out ideas helps clarify their thoughts; they aren't necessarily committing to the ideas they raise.

Impact on others: Extroverted Cacti may acquire a reputation for being untrustworthy.

Who it is most likely to rub the wrong way: Introverted Snowflake

Why? Introverted Snowflakes, who process internally, experience the extroverted Cactus's style as being noncommittal. Hearing them spew forth ideas without following through is interpreted as not keeping their word.

POP QUIZ!
Disconnects *continued*

Tip: Be explicit regarding the difference between a conversation and a contract.

D. Who is most likely to say, "May I join you?" (Followed by plopping down next to you.)

Answer: Extroverted Snowflake

Why? "A stranger is a friend you haven't met yet" is quite nearly their anthem.

Impact on others: People can feel intruded upon.

Most likely to rub the wrong way: Introverted Snowflake

Why? Introverted Snowflakes cherish alone time. Yet to be polite, they'll agree to "being joined."

Tip: Take a page out of your brethren's playbook. Introverted Cacti in the same situation will decline the company by saying, for instance, "I prefer time to myself at the moment." The Snowflake might want to add a little cushion, such as, "Thank you for the offer!"

THE RUBBER HITS THE ROAD
A Privacy Intrusion

Larry, an introverted Cactus, left work on personal leave for three months. His departure was seemingly unexpected and bereft of fanfare. Just as suddenly, he reappeared in a team meeting, without elucidation.

Sue has worked with Larry for a few months and knows he keeps to himself. While not close friends, they are congenial colleagues. She was delighted to see him return.

"Wow, Larry!" she spontaneously gushed. "You're back! Long time no see! We've been worried about you. Where'd you vanish off to?"

She meant well. Yet what was the upshot?

Believe you me, Larry was mortified. He experienced Sue's outburst as an intrusion on his privacy. He felt on the spot, as his introverted protective radar went into overdrive. "Hey, yup, I'm back. Let's get going on the agenda; I've got lots to do."

Sue, an extroverted Snowflake, greeted Larry how *she* would like to be treated when returning from a lengthy absence from work. She hadn't given tremendous thought to her reaction. As an extrovert, she talks to think, and as a Snowflake, she exudes emotion. Still, inner preferences, as we know by now, do not have to dictate behaviors.

If do-over buttons existed (beyond online backgammon), what could Sue have done differently?

Sprinkling the Platinum Rule atop a few useful guidelines would do wonders for Sue's workplace relationships. Let's revisit the same scenario, starting with Larry's sudden reentry into a staff meeting. Here's how the dialogue plays out on Groundhog Day:

Larry: [Nods at his colleagues.]

Sue: Hey Larry, good to see you.

Larry: Ditto.

Meeting commences.

What was the basis of Sue's superstar redo? The effervescent "plan, breathe, calibrate" system. Coming right up.

TOOLSHED MOMENT
Plan, Breathe, Calibrate

There are three simple steps, customized here for Sue.

PLAN. While Larry is on leave, consider how to greet him upon return.

BREATHE. Pause between inner response and outer manifestations of reactions, providing an opportunity to consciously modify.

CALIBRATE. Modify her style to match Larry's preferred modes of interactions.

VIDEO CONFERENCING AND YOU

Upon the onset of COVID-19, use of Zoom and related platforms exploded. In December 2019 Zoom had ten million users, catapulting to three hundred million by December 2020. Rather than delve into their business model, lament missed investment triumphs, or muse about the collision of office space and the pandemic, let's stick with the matter of video conferencing and personalities.

Overall, the extrovert is a decidedly bigger fan of video meetings than the introvert. The allure of group connectivity syncs particularly well with the extroverted Snowflake's personality.

What energizes one person drains another. We each have individual needs and specific methods for recharging. Realizing this while honoring others' requirements ultimately benefits everyone.

The term "Zoom fatigue" resonates mostly with introverted Snowflakes. This is rooted in exhaustion from continually being "on," accompanied by a hesitancy to hurt others' feelings. While introverted Cacti get burned out, they are unapologetic about bowing out whenever possible.

Introverted Snowflakes are gifted at deciphering nonverbals, yet this asset has diminished value in virtual gatherings. It is alarmingly easy to misread body language transmitted via a box within a screen.

Connectivity at Meetings

Each of the four combinations has distinct preferences for how to establish relationships in virtual and live programs.

Introverted Snowflake	→ Pairs to get to know each other
Extroverted Snowflake	→ Groups to get to know each other
Introverted Cactus	→ Pairs to resolve a team challenge
Extroverted Cactus	→ Groups to resolve a team challenge

What to do? Cultivate a heightened understanding of diverse needs. Ask about and respond to preferences when arranging calls and meetings.

UPS AND DOWNS

Let's summarize some behaviors and challenges we might expect to encounter with each combo.

EXTROVERTED SNOWFLAKE

Verbal and emotional, particularly when sharing feelings. Frequent online postings flow forth, with few filters. While well intentioned, may inadvertently break confidentiality.

EXTROVERTED CACTUS

Freely shares opinions, regardless of whether congruent with others in the vicinity. An open, unfiltered communication style can unintentionally create strife. Often unaware if saying something hurtful, meaning no ill will.

INTROVERTED SNOWFLAKE

Reserved and private until a dearly held belief is called into question—resulting in a startlingly strong reaction. Avoids group gatherings unless absolutely mandated or extraordinarily compelling. Maintains an escape route until the last moment.

INTROVERTED CACTUS

Very loyal to a small group of friends. Anti-meetings. Seeks opportunities to gain knowledge and prefers to do so by reading rather than in a group environment. Could use help in gracefully rejecting invitations to events.

An introverted Cactus client confided in me: "I feel like my whole introverted life has been preparing me for an order to stay home and avoid people. I'm loving it!"

POP QUIZ!
The Danger of Dishing

True or False? Casual work emailing and texting is harmless.

Answer: False-o-roni!

Messaging from work or on work accounts can turn into a real mess. It is not melodramatic to say that apparently innocuous activity can result in disaster. Certain personality combinations are at a relatively higher risk for torpedoing an otherwise smooth career trajectory.

HAZARD ALERT: MESSAGING!

Extroverted Snowflakes! Be exceedingly careful how you message. Beware of an unprofessional tone in professional emails, texts, and other forms of messaging.

CAUTION #1

Introverts have a much lower bar for what they consider personal than extroverts.

CAUTION #2

Many workplaces have access to emails and may flag what you innocently intended as a lighthearted joke. A colleague of mine, well respected in his agency, was permanently reassigned because his casual banter was deemed inappropriate.

> ## HAZARD ALERT: MESSAGING! *continued*
>
> ### CAUTION #3
> Regardless of intentions, never forward an email without permission. I've seen careers derailed this way. Don't try to decide which emails are okay to forward and which are not. Eliminate the decision point by never doing it. This tidbit can save you immeasurable headaches down the road.

COMMONALITIES

Whew! We've convinced ourselves that there are ample differences among extroverts, introverts, Cacti, and Snowflakes. We are nervously aware of the dangers lurking in the corners of missteps. We'd be amiss to breeze past our commonalities.

When making a new acquaintance, unless preceded by a briefing, we generally know nil about their defining persona. What to do? These four guideposts work for us all:

- Stay focused.

- Be authentic.

- Convey positivity.

- Seek ways to be helpful.

At the very least, keep your hair in control and your smile sincere.

> **CHEAT SHEET**
>
> - Cactus introverts: Love to process.
> - Cactus extroverts: Love to spar.
> - Snowflake introverts: Love diving deep.
> - Snowflake extroverts: Love to engage.

CHAPTER NINE

Beyond Business

SNOWFLAKES & CACTI
IN YOUR PERSONAL LIFE

*If only you could sense how important you are to the lives
of those you meet; how important you can be to people
you never even dream of. There is something of yourself
that you leave at every meeting with another person.*

—FRED ROGERS

You may ask yourself, *Does this Cactus and Snowflake
stuff ring true above and beyond one's professional life?*
Absolutely.

POP QUIZ!
Pass the Popcorn

Q: Why does a quintessential Flaker persist in watching very
sad documentaries?

A: As she explains: "It's just so satisfying to watch people
overcome adversity!"

PERSONAL MATTERS

In our professional life, we're often called upon to flex our style. Off-duty, we are freer to relax into our core nature. Yet even outside of work, it behooves us to accommodate others at times.

Personal lives are populated with their own cast of characters. Some merit leading roles, others flash by as mere cameos. Those we reckon with beyond the workplace run the gamut: significant others, immediate family, extended family, roommates, friends, acquaintances, neighbors, and fellow members of community organizations.

The more time we spend with any particular individual, the more opportunities to grate on each others' nerves. I've heard it said that the only normal people are the ones we don't know very well. Quirks amplify over time. Personality differences contribute to this phenomenon.

TOOLSHED MOMENT
Cohabitation Conundrums

If you dwell in a personality-diverse household, you already know the vast disparity between how behaviors can be intended and how they may be interpreted. Allow me to offer up four illustrations of how this may play out.

EVENT ONE

Cactus gets up and goes into another room. What happened?

Snowflake: The Cactus is being rude and insensitive.

Cactus: Nothing.

EVENT TWO

Cactus enters the room while on the phone. Does not make eye contact or nod in greeting. What happened?

Snowflake: The Cactus is angry at me, and therefore ignoring me.

Cactus: I was talking on the phone.

EVENT THREE

Snowflake joins Cactus relaxing on the couch. What happened?

Snowflake: I'm seizing an opportunity for quality time.

Cactus: My time to unwind was interrupted. Now it's gone.

EVENT FOUR

Snowflake asks what's on Cactus's mind. Cactus responds, "Nothing." What happened?

Snowflake: Cactus doesn't want me to know what they are thinking.

Cactus: I answered a question.

As you may have experienced firsthand, any of these vast divides can inspire a brawl.

To add insult to injury, all the delineated points of view are arguable. That means they rely on subjective analysis rather than tangible data. While we can agree you entered the room on the phone, no one can prove whether you were consciously ignoring me. If we're looking to identify a winner, we're out of luck.

How to gracefully move forward?

Let's start with the premise you're not always right. Okay, scratch that. For argument's sake, we'll agree that you *are* always right. How important is that to you? Are there any desired outcomes that supersede rightness? Or for that matter, winning? Any of these, ever?

- A peaceful home
- A happy "other person"
- Moving on
- Letting go
- Being helpful
- Personal growth
- Bigger fish to fry

Practice this line of thought and you may come to the conclusion that being right is overrated.

THE RUBBER HITS THE ROAD

Parking Lot Meltdown

My colleague Reggie shared a vignette from a holiday with his wife, Latoya. While Reggie is a stalwart Snowflake, Latoya is a certified Cactus. Due to COVID-19, they had not traveled for months. Given a cautiously optimistic outlook, with health trends on the upswing, they decided on a three-day mini vacation at a lightly populated state park. It was a modest destination, within easy driving distance.

They agreed beforehand on what they would and would not do to ensure a maximum mutual comfort level. Before hitting the road, they carefully mapped out policies regarding masks, pit stops, and hand sanitizer usage. Latoya offered to write up their plan and did so in meticulous detail. With ample camping gear and plenty of food, they embarked on their outing, thrilled by the projected forecast of mild weather. Everything proceeded smoothly until the final hours.

Weary of simultaneously grainy and watery campfire coffee, on day three they noticed a humble string of shops featuring a café with locally made java. They skidded into the parking lot and jumped out of their Prius.

It wasn't until exiting the car that Reggie noticed the relatively high volume of humanity surrounding them. Even while donning masks, and with an average of ten feet between themselves and others, Reggie—in his own words—"freaked out." He broke into a cold sweat and began snapping at Latoya to "get back in the vehicle."

Latoya would have none of it. She calmly reached into the glove compartment and pulled out their policy statement. They were well within the limits of agreed-upon safety levels. What was the problem? She strolled toward the tantalizing wafts emanating from the café.

In the recesses of his mind, Reggie knew Latoya was accurately interpreting their carefully worded rational framework. Technically, he also knew that they were abiding with these guidelines. This all had zero impact on his inner state. He fortressed himself in the car, glaring at the horizon.

When recollecting the episode from the safety of his home, he agreed that Latoya's behavior was rational. He later laughed about his reaction. But at the time, consumed by vague, imprecise feelings, Reggie felt inarticulate and overwhelmed. Latoya's response entailed, in part, reciting the decision points they made as a family prior to travel. She explained the logic, offering up practical explanations so he would relax. Needless to say, he did not.

It's hard to say who was more frustrated. What *is* clear? Neither convinced the other to experience things differently.

The way of the world in the Arctic Circle is entirely disparate from life in the Sahara Desert. The natural habitats of Snowflakes and Cacti couldn't be more distinct. Yet here we are, living side by side, sometimes in very close quarters. Navigating our shared experiences. Experiences that run the gamut from cooking a meal to organizing a room to . . . home-based Zoom (or the like) events.

I imagine you've attended at least one virtual event in your personal life. High school reunion. Alumni gathering. Celebratory party. Stay-at-home game night.

With higher frequencies of virtual gatherings, new opportunities arise. Or as a Cactus might put it, "New opportunities for implosions!"

Virtual Family Reunion

In a moment of confusion, you decide to organize a virtual family reunion. Perhaps you were in an altered state of consciousness. I will ask no follow-up questions. In solidarity, however, I will provide a roadmap to smooth the way.

Invitations

Do: Confirm correct contact information.
Do not: Blind cc as these are likely to enter spam.
Do not: Feel compelled to invite the entire family tree.
Do: Ask for volunteers to put together a slideshow or activity.

Cactus at the Helm

Select a master of ceremony. Otherwise, brace yourself for a meandering, tedious event dominated by a small portion of participants. I nominate you, or a designated Cactus of your choice, for this role. If you're a Snowflake, you may want to strategically delegate out certain don't-mess-with-me components.

Prior to Go-Time

Many virtual gatherings morph into a mountain of technical difficulties. Be proactive. Offer advance help. Also invite suspected Luddites or self-proclaimed technophobes to join fifteen minutes early to iron out snafus. Factoring in this pre-event cushion, by ten minutes into the event you needn't continue troubleshooting. The purpose of the gathering is to connect, not to run a tech seminar.

As a corollary, *when* (not *if*, it's inevitable) folks join in late, you needn't recap everything that has already occurred. You snooze, you lose. No point in reprimanding latecomers either. They can slide into the gathering without making a ruckus.

Structure

Depending on the group's size, a solid starting point is providing each person with one to two minutes to share highlights of what's been going on in their neck of the woods. Have a timer handy. Again, this is where Cacti excel. I suggest sounding a bell tone when time is up, letting them finish the current sentence. Believe me, it nips rambling in the bud and makes you a hero.

Next, facilitate activities to help members reconnect and enjoy themselves—a family trivia contest, sharing funny memories, a guessing game, or talent show. Choose a subsection of these to mention in the invitations. At last count, there are a zillion zany activities that can be conducted virtually. Or simply prepare a few lighthearted questions, provided in advance. Without structure, there will be some who haven't spoken a word by the event's conclusion.

Steer clear of topics that interest a limited subsection of attendees, such as minutiae pertaining to one's offspring or pampered pets. This is at best boring and at worst insensitive. I implore you to squelch such yawn-inducers immediately.

Snowflake's Emotional Preparation
Take some deep breaths. Regardless of how pro-reunion you are on the Richter Scale, there's a fifty-one percent chance your feelings will be inadvertently hurt at some point during the event. As we both know, you are capable of reading into *anything*. I will not come out and use the term *hypersensitive*, because we're both hypersensitive to that term. Suffice to say, in all likelihood no offense was intended. Let it slide, squeeze a stress ball, and redirect your attention.

Cactus's Practical Preparation
Prepare yourself. At some point, regardless of how successful the event, somebody will grate on your nerves. Smooth sailing is statistically improbable. Even within a structured format, virtual reunions have haphazard moments, and you have a pretty strong idea about who's at fault. Plan a strategy in advance to stay in check at game time. Doodling, perhaps? Restrain yourself from blurting out a snide remark.

What is hilarious to you is a ruinous comment to another. Let it slide, throw some office darts, and redirect your attention.

Wrap It Up

Upon conclusion, allow participants to make offers to the group—say, providing talents (such as resume help), donating items, or organizing future events. Mention this briefly at the very end, so the conversations do not devolve into lengthy diatribes. Specifics can be handled privately by the interested parties. End on time rather than letting things wane unceremoniously. As my grandfather would say, "Leave while you're still having fun."

The Aftermath

Don't bombard unsuspecting attendees with strings of follow-up messaging. Refrain from using Reply All in group emails. Nothing ruins a reunion like an afterparty without borders. The beauty of nonwork events is that attendance is not required. You're not obligated to join follow-up gatherings just because you received an invite. Look out for yourself and your energy levels.

Note: Naturally, these tips can all be applied to numerous types of virtual gatherings.

THE RUBBER HITS THE ROAD

Harvest Delivery

Carla was invited by her neighbor to sign up for a CSA (community-supported agriculture) subscription, wherein a fresh-from-the-farm harvest would be delivered to her doorstep for a reasonable fee. She didn't know the farmer was her neighbor's best friend and beta-testing her business. The initial basket arrived several hours late, with all the promised vegetables missing in action. In their stead was an odd, wrinkled assortment of items she didn't want and barely recognized. The accompanying "floral bouquet" was a massive clump of drooping flowers, roots and soil included. Once she brought them inside, she discovered they were also infested with an array of insects.

Cactus, what would you have done? That's right. Depending on the scope of the mishap, you might ask for a replacement or refund. You would certainly discontinue the service, telling the farmer what was unsatisfactory about the delivery. You would neither apologize (what on earth for?) nor experience guilt. Just mild to moderate annoyance.

While Carla mulled over her response, she was contacted to write a review of the "Farm to Family" delivery service. She couldn't be disingenuous and give a rave review. Yet she didn't want to be denigrating, potentially harming a fledgling business that might improve over time. After much angst she declined to post a review and reverted to visiting a seasonal produce stand down the road.

Is there a Snowflake in proximity? What would be your reaction if in Carla's shoes?

POP QUIZ!
How Snowy are you?

Let's bring it home. What if you were at the receiving end of the CSA's misguided delivery attempt?

Select from the following options, checking any that apply.

POSSIBLE REACTIONS

☐	Feel bad for the proprietor.
☐	Hope you didn't look disappointed when accepting the delivery.
☐	Experience stress about how to handle it.
☐	Consider giving the service another chance.
☐	Wonder if you were unclear when placing your order.
☐	Ask yourself, *What did I expect? She's new at this.*
☐	Offer a reason that circumvents blame, decline future service.

5–7 checks   You are a classic Snowflake

2–4 checks   You're a moderate Snowflake—*or*—you flex your style

0–1 checks   You're midway between Snowflake and Cactus *or*—you flex your style

This is about knowing yourself, rather than discerning the proper response. The more you understand your unique outlook and expectations, the more choices you have.

Periodically remind yourself that you don't get a vote on others' choices.

Jackpot! The rest of us don't get a vote on your life designs either.

THE RUBBER HITS THE ROAD
All In

Among a small cluster of her lifelong friends, Tamara is the sole Snowflake and most introverted. She is the least likely to chime in on group messages or join remote gatherings. As holiday time was fast approaching, she mentioned being open to a video call. Perhaps they could set something up over the next few weeks? Unexpectedly, the others responded that they already had one scheduled for that very evening, and why didn't Tamara join in?

Tamara felt a stabbing sensation, hurt to have been excluded from the original plan. She told herself, *I bet this happens all the time. They probably don't want me around.* Bookshelves of self-doubt crashed all around her.

Tamara joined the video call regardless, which they specially rearranged to fit her needs. Despite her inner drama, it proceeded swimmingly. Her friends explained their intention was to respect Tamara, knowing she typically shies away from group get-togethers. She grudgingly realized it had slipped her mind that when they had invited her several times previously, she had categorically declined the offers.

Tamara got two takeaways.

First: Her Cacti friends exhibited transparency by not hesitating to tell Tamara that a meeting was already in place without her knowledge. They had nothing to hide and no ill will. It was a testament to their friendship that it hadn't even occurred to them to pretend otherwise.

Second: Tamara considered how she might have behaved if the shoe were on the other foot. More likely than not, Tamara would have considered a white lie to keep the peace. She later realized it would be disingenuous to cover up a pre-game plan in the name of being nice.

In the preceding scenario, Tamara had several choices to make. This brings to mind the eternal question: Who makes better decisions, Snowflakes or Cacti? Turns out, neither camp has the market cornered on successful decision making. This really irks the Cacti . . . behind closed doors they will continue the debate.

The crux of the matter is not the quality of decisions, but the underlying methodology. Snowflakes will rely on their feelings, hunches, perceptions, and sentiments. Cacti will rely on data, cognition, logic, and facts. Here's the rub. When either follows their natural style, they both make wiser choices than when they attempt to decide "out of type." Many Snowflakes have told me that when they make significant life decisions based on what's logical, they nearly always regret it.

THE RUBBER HITS THE ROAD

Discerning What Matters

Homeowner associations (HOAs) are typi-
cally filled to the brim with Cacti. Members are called upon to manage disagreements, mitigate conflicting interests, and argue over priorities. All attractions for those with a

tough exterior. Here's a saga from an HOA for a group of townhomes.

It was late spring, and the star amenity—the neighborhood pool—was slated to open Memorial Day weekend, as usual. Yet this year the HOA ran into some mishaps, ranging from unresponsive pool maintenance contractors to a shift in lifeguard providers. It didn't help that they got a late start due to poorly planned vacation schedules. Deadlines came and went.

The Board of Directors began to receive a flurry of emails asking questions they couldn't answer, so they did not reply. In mid-June the pool remained closed. The officers redirected their attention toward updating the HOA website. They threw themselves into this more manageable project with gusto, eschewing their residents' more significant and pressing needs.

This dedicated group of mostly retired volunteers cared about their community, yet they lost track of what mattered most. Who craved the pool most desperately? Young parents, unable to dedicate time to a forceful campaign amid the endless demands of their taxing lives. Many had moved into the community largely for the attraction of the pool.

No action was made on the pool—or at least nothing was communicated. On a bright, sunny, perfect swimming weather day in late June, there was an email blast proudly proclaiming, "We are thrilled to debut . . . our new state-of-the art website!"

The announcement was not received with the anticipated acclaim. Residents were infuriated. "*This* is what you've been spending your time, energy, and attention on? We don't give a _____ [fill in the blank] about a website. We need our pool!"

The good news? Plenty of broadly applicable lessons were learned. New protocols were established. And the pool eventually opened.

LESSONS GLEANED
Seek a Mixed Crowd
A mix of Snowflakes and Cacti is nearly always more effective than a group populated with one type. In this case, merging structure with sensitivity would have kept the HOA on track. And I said "nearly" only because I haven't conducted an in-depth study of every group everywhere. Deadlines, people.

Learn What Matters
Exit your bubble to learn what is important to others. We tend to gravitate toward like-minded groups. If you're surrounded by Snowflakes, make an effort to visit the Cactus Garden.

Seek out windows into what the Snowflake or Cactus next door values. This enables you to be inclusive in your efforts. Surveys are your friend.

Communicate
You needn't have all the answers. Listen and respond to stated concerns. Acknowledging feelings goes a long way with Snowflakes. Understanding the logic behind decisions mobilizes Cacti.

Anticipate Bumps in the Road
Create cushions for unanticipated setbacks. Beats getting flummoxed and abandoning ship.

Clarify Priorities

The HOA website was on the list. It just wasn't top of the list.

Do a reality check. When unclear about where to direct your energy, ask yourself *Am I fixing up a website when what's needed is a pool?*

- Give others the benefit of the doubt.

- Maintain perspective. Keep in mind what matters most.

- Pave a solid foundation for life beyond the workplace.

CONCLUSION

Don't bend; don't water it down; don't try to make it logical; don't edit your own soul according to the fashion. Rather, follow your most intense obsessions mercilessly.

—FRANZ KAFKA

POP QUIZ!
Philosophically Speaking

Here are two philosophers and their defining principles. Cover up—or otherwise avoid—the answers while taking the brief quiz.

1. Martin Buber

Premise: Strive for quality relationships (as embodied by his *I and Thou* driving principle).

Life is about the creation of meaningful encounters; strive to elevate all interactions.

2. Ludwig Wittgenstein

Premise: Life centers on intellectual tension, with confusion based in linguistic concepts.

Interactions are arranged in social constructs.

Based on this limited information:

Which is a Cactus? _____

Which is a Snowflake? _____

Buber = Snowflake
Wittgenstein = Cactus.

Raise your hand if you assessed correctly.

I knew it. I knew you would!

DEVORA'S QUICKIE TIPPIES

Here are a few guidelines for navigating challenges:

- Perceived liabilities hold the key to your finest strengths.

- Enjoy life. Get a kick out of endearing little eccentricities, including your own.

- Practice the tools woven throughout this book.

Next . . .

- Replace judgment with curiosity and compassion.

- Notice others. Listen, observe, learn, adapt.

Then . . .

- Get to know those on both sides of the spectrum. You'll be glad you did.

WORKSHEET: Spot the Style

Now that you're approaching expert status, you know how thoroughly Cacti and Snowflakes infuse the ether. The philosopher pop quiz was a warmup. Are you on the lookout for a no-cost hobby? Be on alert for examples past and present, with any backdrop. I call it "Spot the Style." Let's give it a go.

Which style said each of the following? These are all real statements, transcribed verbatim.

1. "I always say yes when asked to do a favor, because I'm a nice person."_____

2. "Why don't you make decisions based on what makes the most sense?" _____

3. "You can't say 'don't be offended' . . . it doesn't work that way." _____

4. "It helps to not have delicate feelings and have the ability to ignore silly stuff." _____

5. "We are here to feel. That is the point of living."_____

6. "It is what it is."_____

The next section is comparative.

7. "The main point of a conversation is to get a sense of connection."_____

8. "The main point of a conversation is to exchange information." _____

9. "The most important thing is inclusion." _____

WORKSHEET: Spot the Style *continued*

10. "The most important thing is precision." _____

11. "Collaboration is a strategy." _____

12. "Collaboration is an art form." _____

Response to a contractor unceremoniously quitting a home repair job midway:

13. "It really stinks. This is a major inconvenience." _____

14. "It really stinks. I had such a good feeling about him." _____

Admonishment to a person not wearing a protective mask during the COVID-19 pandemic:

15. "You made people uncomfortable." _____

16. "You broke the law." _____

17. Slogan sighted on a moving company's truck:

   "The Movers Who Care" _____

Answers: 1. Snowflake 2. Cactus 3. Snowflake 4. Cactus 5. Snowflake 6. Cactus 7. Snowflake 8. Cactus 9. Snowflake 10. Cactus 11. Cactus 12. Snowflake 13. Cactus 14. Snowflake 15. Snowflake 16. Cactus 17. Snowflake

OPENING THE FLOOR FOR Q&A

It's been a pleasure presenting to you. I'll now open the floor for questions and points of clarification. Oops, this is a book. No prob, Bob. I've assembled a list of top Frequently Asked Questions (FAQ) posed to me on the covered topics.

FAQ

1. Don't all people think *and* feel? How can we label people as *either* Cacti or Snowflakes?

   Yes, that is an astute observation. Indeed, everyone thinks and feels! Yet there are gradations of how strongly one relates to and identifies with each operative style. Some are off-the-chart, others are a near-even mix. Most have an affinity for one dimension over the other. For ease of use, we create two primary clusters, knowing there are degrees of affiliation.

2. What if my *Cacflake Instrument* results (chapter 1) don't ring true to me? I believe I'm a different primary style than the score indicates.

   This happens at times. Mismatches between results and self-perception can arise, particularly when the assessment was completed by considering learned behaviors rather than core preferences. For example, you may be a very sensitive person who has learned to be tougher on the job. If your results don't make sense to you, retake the self-assessment while keeping in mind what you prefer rather than how you have taught yourself to adapt to various circumstances.

3. Are personalities learned or innate?

   Foundational preferences are innate. That means your temperament is part of your essence. This does not limit you. You are in charge of your proficiencies, including the ability to cultivate aptitudes you deem important.

Plenty of people become so adept at modeling from an opposite style that the casual observer would never recognize this as learned behavior.

Remember: Acquiring new behaviors is not correlated with shifting innate penchants.

4. Do people flip from one side of the spectrum to the other?

Sometimes. It depends. If you exhibit a slight preference, it would not be extraordinary to cross through the middle regularly. Otherwise, most folks are fairly consistent in their temperament. If you exhibit a strong preference, it is unlikely you will "type out" as the reverse style next time you take an assessment.

Let's be clear: We can learn adaptive behaviors, as noted in the response to #3. This doesn't alter who we are deep inside.

5. What is *flexing your style*, and why does it matter?

Flexing means meeting others where they're at. Expecting others to meet us halfway is foolhardy and certain to frustrate. Most people are not skilled enough to traverse the terrain to flex toward us. That makes it our job.

Flexing matters because Flakers and Cacti are frequently motivated by disparate drivers. Hone your skill at picking up on others' subtle clues and enjoy a lifetime of building rapport, increasing productivity, and enhancing life satisfaction. That's all.

6. What's the basis of the Snowflake/Cactus paradigm and how pervasive is it?

The personality dimension highlighted in this book is rooted in Carl Jung's typology and the four cognitive functions. In particular, the concepts underlying our Snowflake and Cactus premise are based on his identification of the Thinker—Feeler spectrum.

Personalities that lead with the head or the heart traverse the globe. How distinctive natures manifest culturally differs according to societal norms.

Keeping your binoculars handy, discover how thoroughly Snowflakes and Cacti permeate the nooks and crannies of our lives.

PRIORITIES

As we near the end, the big question is, *Where to begin?* I've just thrown a lot of stuff at you. You might want to tidy up a bit.

As our journey together concludes, it's time to venture out on your own. With all these tips, tools, suggestions, and admonishments, what is a person to do?

My advice (I thought you'd never ask!) is to start with one or two priorities. Base your selection on what jumped out the most from these pages. I understand it can be a bit stressful to integrate new ideas into your wheelhouse. I'll offer up a quote that I reference frequently. It's the gift that keeps on giving, from author Henry Miller:

> **"Don't be nervous. Work calmly, joyously, recklessly on whatever is in hand."**

I believe in you.

WHEN ALL IS SAID AND DONE

Keep this tucked away for safekeeping . . .

There is much we can learn from each other. We all have predispositions, tendencies, and irksome quirks. We each embody a little bit of our own opposite. No one has cornered the market on being human.

When in doubt . . .
Look out for one another.

And finally . . .
Accept yourself.

That's a radical suggestion. Sit with it a bit. I'll brew you some whole leaf tea.

The Cactus & Snowflake at Work

DISCUSSION & REFLECTION GUIDE

Following are prompts for further reflection on concepts introduced in *The Cactus & Snowflake at Work*. They work well in the context of discussion groups, book clubs, individual self-reflection, and journaling.

Readers are also highly encouraged to engage in the interactive components of the book, such as *Pop Quizzes*, *Worksheets*, *Toolshed Moments*, and—of course—the *Cacflake Instrument* personality assessment.

Why do you think the author swapped out the traditional terminology of *Thinker* and *Feeler* for *Cactus* and *Snowflake*? What was the impact of this choice on you?

What did you think—or how did you feel—about your *Cacflake Instrument* results?

The book has many *Rubber Hits the Road* real-life scenarios. Do you have a *Rubber Hits the Road* example that sheds light on how personality influences your own interactions?

Dissipating stereotypes is thematically woven throughout the book. Did reading this book break down some of your own previously held assumptions?

Several examples of *Hazard Alerts* are provided for each personality style. What are hazards you've faced while interacting with those different from you? How did you overcome these potential hazards?

How has implementing the *Big Two* been useful?
[Reminder: 1. Observe; 2. Ask]

Reflect back on a time when your experience of an event varied wildly with that of another person involved. Do you now think it could have been a quintessential *Nonevent* (NE)? What fresh perspective can the NE concept offer in future encounters?

The Cactus & Snowflake at Work insists you can directly influence only three things: your thoughts, words, and actions. How does this link to the acronym *NAY* (not about you)?

"Mind your own business!" is often perceived as a reprimand. Tone certainly comes into play. How does the author repurpose *Mind Your Own Business* as a concept to free readers from focusing on matters beyond their control?

Commit to spending a day with razor-sharp focus on others' language choices. When possible, respond with matching language options.

If you created a mantra while engaging in the book's activities, how has it influenced your self-talk and behaviors?

When have you metaphorically put beans up others' noses? What happens when you instead pause and parse before speaking?

Next time you observe someone seeming to be *In the Grip*, reserve judgment, replace with empathy, and test out the supportive measures offered in the book.

What happens when you have an extreme reaction to an event and follow that up with an exploration of your *meta-state*? How does this tie in to *reframing*?

There are myriad factors contributing to what makes us tick. This book includes an exploration of how introversion and extroversion interplay with the Cactus and Snowflake aspects of personality. Do you believe you are an introvert or extrovert? How does this tie in to your identification as a Cactus or Snowflake?

What one or two lessons or ideas most stand out to you from this book? How have you implemented changes based on these concepts?

Is there someone in your life who seems to reside at the opposite end of the spectrum from you? How do you benefit from this relationship? What can you do to strengthen your connection?

APPENDIX A

Thinker-Feeler Facets

Adapted from the *U.S. Supplement to MBTI Global Manual* (Consulting Psychologist Press, 2018).

THINKER	FEELER
Logical	Empathetic
Reasoning	Compassionate
Questioning	Accommodating
Critical	Accepting
Tough	Tender

APPENDIX B

The Real Deal

Enjoy these fascinating real-world snowflake and cactus tidbits.

SNOWFLAKE FACTS

A snowflake is a six-sided fractal, a complex pattern that repeats itself forever, regardless of size. A branch of geometry called fractal geometry helps explain the figures of snowflakes.

A snowflake's style is determined by the humidity and temperature upon formation. Dendrites form when the air temperature is between −8 and +14 degrees Fahrenheit.

- Snowflakes do not have perfect symmetry.

- Snowflakes fall at a rate of 3.1 miles per hour.

- Each snowflake contains 180 billion to 10 quintillion molecules of water.

- The six basic types of snowflakes are: *flat*, *column*, *stars*, *dendrite*, *lacy*, *needle*, and *capped column*.

CACTUS FACTS

Cactus plants are members of the Cactaceae family. These plants feature succulent stems and branches with spines or scales. They do not have traditional leaf structures. Cacti are generally found in arid climates such as deserts.

Cacti combine a hard protective exterior with strong endurance, enabling survival in drought-like conditions. Their hardiness extends to being adaptive in a range of environments. *Sabra cacti* (Opuntia), also called prickly pear, are known for combining a soft interior with a tough exterior.

- There are 127 genera in the Cactaceae family.

- Some cactus species can survive for two years without water.

- The saguaro cactus (*Carnegiea gigantea*), known for its "arms," is a defining plant of the Sonoran Desert.

- The world's largest cacti species, Mexican cardon (*Pachycereus pringlei*), can live up to three hundred years.

BIBLIOGRAPHY

Don't bother to be better than your contemporaries or predecessors. Try to be better than yourself.

—WILLIAM FAULKNER

Babauta, Leo. *The Power of Less*. Westport, CT: Hyperion, 2009.

Bandler, Richard, and John Grinder. *ReFraming: Neuro-Linguistic Programming and the Transformation of Meaning*. Moab, UT: Real People Press, 1982.

Buber, Martin. *I and Thou*. New York: Touchstone, 1971.

Carr, Nicholas. *The Shallows*. New York: Norton, 2011.

Cashman, Kevin. *The Pause Principle*. Oakland, CA: Berrett-Koehler, 2012.

Czikszentmihalyi, Mihaly. *Flow: The Psychology of Optimal Experience*. New York: HarperCollins, 2008.

Fischer, Roger, and Daniel Shapiro. *Beyond Reason*. New York: Penguin, 2007.

Fischer, Roger, and William Ury. *Getting to Yes*. 2nd ed. New York: Penguin, 2011.

Gladwell, Malcolm. *David and Goliath*. New York: Back Bay Books, 2015.

Goleman, Daniel. *Emotional Intelligence*. New York: Bantam, 2005.

Hoobyar, Tom, Tom Dotz, and Susan Sanders. *NLP: The Essential Guide*. New York: HarperCollins, 2013.

Jiang, Manyu. "The Reason Zoom Calls Drain Your Energy." *BBC*, April 22, 2020. https://www.bbc.com/worklife/article/20200421-why-zoom-video-chats-are-so-exhausting.

Jones, Steve. "No Brown M&M's: What Van Halen's Insane Contract Clause Teaches Entrepreneurs." *Entrepreneur*, March 24, 2014.

Jung, Carl. *Memories, Dreams, Reflections*. New York: Pantheon Books, 1973.

Jung, Carl. *Psychological Types*. Princeton, NJ: Princeton University Press, 1976.

Juster, Norton. *The Phantom Tollbooth*. 35th anniversary ed. New York: Random House, 1989.

Katie, Byron. *Loving What Is*. New York: Harmony Books, 2003.

Kroeger, Otto, and Janet Thuesen. *Type Talk at Work*. 2nd ed. McHenry, IL: Delta, 2002.

Machemer, Theresa. "Why Video Calls Are Surprisingly Exhausting." *Smithsonian*, April 29, 2020. https://www.smithsonianmag.com/smart-news/why-video-calls-are-surprisingly-exhausting-180974773/.

Myers-Briggs Company. *U.S. Supplement to MBTI Global Manual*. Mountain View, CA: Consulting Psychologist Press, 2018.

Pattakos, Alex, PhD. *Prisoners of Our Thoughts*. Oakland, CA: Berrett-Koehler, 2008.

Phillips, Patti, and Jack Phillips. "Measuring the Impact and ROI of Virtual Learning." *Chief Operating Officer*, December 21, 2020.

Quenk, Naomi. *In the Grip: Understanding Type, Stress, and the Inferior Function*. 2nd ed. Windsor, CO: CPP Inc., 2000.

Wittgenstein, Ludwig. *Philosophical Investigations*, 4th ed. West Sussex, United Kingdom: Wiley-Blackwell, 2009.

Zack, Devora. *Managing for People Who Hate Managing*. Oakland, CA: Berrett-Koehler/ASTD Press, 2012.

Zack, Devora. *Networking for People Who Hate Networking*. 2nd ed. Oakland, CA: Berrett-Koehler, 2019.

Zack, Devora. *Singletasking*. Oakland, CA: Berrett-Koehler, 2015.

ACKNOWLEDGMENTS

Love one another and you will be happy. It's as simple and as difficult as that.

—MICHAEL LEUNIG

My endless appreciation to all the Snowflakes and Cacti who inspired this book. You know your whereabouts. I respect your thoughts and feelings in equal parts, and ideally have buoyed some spirits along the way.

Thank you to my exemplary reviewers: Chloe Lizotte, Chloe Park, and Candace Sinclair, and fastidious copy editor: Kristi Hein. Appreciation to Seventeenth Street Studios for going above and beyond. Huge gratitude to my dedicated, dueling editors Jeevan and Neal. Thanks again, Jeevan, for discovering me at that conference so long ago. Also, appreciation goes out to the marvelous Berrett-Koehler team and community, which at some point transformed into my family.

Super special gratitude to the four guys and two cockatiels who share our cozy home. Your patience, encouragement, support, enthusiasm, love, humor, and bright cheer ensured this book's creation.

INDEX

A
actions
    flexing style and, 79
    mantra and, 84–85
    personally relevant benefits
      and, 81–86
adaptability, 40, 106
affirmation, 95
agreement, 43–44
alternative realities, 50–52
annual performance review,
    114–116

B
beans up the nose, 64–66
behaviors, reasons behind,
    26–30
Buber, Martin, 153

C
Cacflake Instrument, 3–4, 10–18,
    157
Cactus
    actions and, 79
conflict and, 58
    defining characteristics,
      20–26
    as insult, 5
    leadership characteristics,
      106–107, 111
    living with Snowflake,
      138–139
    as matter of degree, 8–10
    moderate preference for, in
      Cacflake, 15–16

perks, 32
praise and, 107–108
propensities, 32
rudeness and, 58–60
shadow style, 94, 95
slight preference for, in
    Cacflake, 15
stereotypes, 22–23
strong preference for, in
    Cacflake, 16
tone and, 61–63
words, 76
"clicking," with others, 83
Close, Chuck, 105
cohabitation, 138–139
conflict
conversation vs., 57–64
    nonevent and, 50
conversation, conflict vs., 57–64
COVID-19, 132

D
defining characteristics, 20–26
diplomacy, 80
directness, 80
discussion guide, 161–163

E
emotional separation, 102
extroversion. See introversion/
    extroversion (I/E)

F
family reunion, virtual, 142–146
feedback, 83, 112–118

172

ABOUT DEVORA

*I've written thousands of words that no one will ever see.
I had to write them in order to get rid of them.*

—RAY BRADBURY

Devora is a best-selling author, global keynote speaker, leadership consultant, and executive coach. Her internationally released books, *Networking for People Who Hate Networking*, *Singletasking*, and *Managing for People Who Hate Managing*, are in forty-five language translations. Awards include *Forbes* Top Networking book 2019, *Forbes* Top Five Self-Help Books, *Wealth Management* Top Five Business Books of 2015, and Top Ten Non-Fiction by the *Washington Post*.

Devora loves writing yet deplores deadlines. She has discovered that gazing out the window while intermittently deleting sentences is not as romantic a profession as it initially appears. She has no idea why she keeps forgetting this valuable lesson. Theories are welcome. Hope reigns supreme that you'll personally benefit from her faulty memory.

She has degrees from University of Pennsylvania (BA) and Cornell University (MBA), memberships in Phi Beta Kappa and Mensa, and is a certified practitioner in Neuro-Linguistic Programming (NLP) and Myers-Briggs Type Indicator (MBTI). She has a vague sense that no one takes her particularly seriously and hopes listing these credentials will help in some small way.

Devora loves to kayak, cook, eat, exaggerate, and break a sweat.

That sums up the highlights of what there is to know about our foolhardy yet trusty author.

ONLY CONNECT CONSULTING

Learn the rules like a pro so you can break them like an artist.

—PABLO PICASSO

Only Connect Consulting (OCC) is an international leadership development firm with 100+ clients. OCC has grown annually for twenty-five years as an entirely referral-based business. Clients hail from the tundra to the desert, including the Smithsonian, Australian Institute of Management, Pfizer, London Business School, National Institutes of Health, FDA, Mensa, U.S. Department of the Interior, Delta Airlines, U.S. Patent and Trademark Office, and Johns Hopkins Medical Institute.

Devora, OCC's CEO, has been featured in dozens of media such as *The Wall Street Journal, USA Today, ABC-TV, Bloomberg Radio, U.S. News & World Report, CNN Money, CNBC, Fox News, British Airways Magazine, Forbes, Cosmo, Self, Redbook, Women's Health, Working Mother, CEO,* and *Fast Company.*

Enjoy selected interviews and articles at: myonlyconnect.com.

Make inquiries for custom programs and speaking engagements: connect@myonlyconnect.com.

Also by Devora Zack

Networking for People Who Hate Networking

A Field Guide for Introverts, the Overwhelmed, and the Underconnected, Second Edition

Would you rather get a root canal than schmooze with a bunch of strangers? Does the phrase "working a room" make you want to retreat to yours? Is small talk a big problem? Devora Zack used to be just like you—in fact, she still is. An avowed introvert, she's also a successful consultant who addresses thousands of people each year, and she didn't change her personality to do it. Quite the contrary. You don't have to become a backslapping extrovert or even learn how to fake it. She shows you how the very traits that make you hate networking can be harnessed to forge an approach even more effective than traditional techniques. It's a different kind of networking—and it works.

Paperback, 208 pages, ISBN 978-1-5230-9853-8
PDF ebook, ISBN 978-1-5230-9854-5
ePub book ISBN 978-1-5230-9855-2
Digital audio ISBN 978-1-5230-9852-1

Berrett–Koehler Publishers, Inc.
www.bkconnection.com

800.929.2929

Berrett–Koehler
Publishers

Berrett-Koehler is an independent publisher dedicated to an ambitious mission: *Connecting people and ideas to create a world that works for all.*

Our publications span many formats, including print, digital, audio, and video. We also offer online resources, training, and gatherings. And we will continue expanding our products and services to advance our mission.

We believe that the solutions to the world's problems will come from all of us, working at all levels: in our society, in our organizations, and in our own lives. Our publications and resources offer pathways to creating a more just, equitable, and sustainable society. They help people make their organizations more humane, democratic, diverse, and effective (and we don't think there's any contradiction there). And they guide people in creating positive change in their own lives and aligning their personal practices with their aspirations for a better world.

And we strive to practice what we preach through what we call "The BK Way." At the core of this approach is *stewardship,* a deep sense of responsibility to administer the company for the benefit of all of our stakeholder groups, including authors, customers, employees, investors, service providers, sales partners, and the communities and environment around us. Everything we do is built around stewardship and our other core values of *quality, partnership, inclusion,* and *sustainability.*

This is why Berrett-Koehler is the first book publishing company to be both a B Corporation (a rigorous certification) and a benefit corporation (a for-profit legal status), which together require us to adhere to the highest standards for corporate, social, and environmental performance. And it is why we have instituted many pioneering practices (which you can learn about at www.bkconnection.com), including the Berrett-Koehler Constitution, the Bill of Rights and Responsibilities for BK Authors, and our unique Author Days.

We are grateful to our readers, authors, and other friends who are supporting our mission. We ask you to share with us examples of how BK publications and resources are making a difference in your lives, organizations, and communities at www.bkconnection.com/impact.

Dear reader,

Thank you for picking up this book and welcome to the worldwide BK community! You're joining a special group of people who have come together to create positive change in their lives, organizations, and communities.

What's BK all about?

Our mission is to connect people and ideas to create a world that works for all.

Why? Our communities, organizations, and lives get bogged down by old paradigms of self-interest, exclusion, hierarchy, and privilege. But we believe that can change. That's why we seek the leading experts on these challenges—and share their actionable ideas with you.

A welcome gift

To help you get started, we'd like to offer you a **free copy** of one of our bestselling ebooks:

www.bkconnection.com/welcome

When you claim your **free ebook**, you'll also be subscribed to our blog.

Our freshest insights

Access the best new tools and ideas for leaders at all levels on our blog at ideas.bkconnection.com.

Sincerely,

Your friends at Berrett-Koehler